the handmade paper book

angela ramsay

photography by emma peios

To my 'quartet' of sons: Mark, Pete, Achaladeva and Sacanâma.
To my 'trio' of grandchildren: Kirsten, Rachael and Fraser and to those not 'composed' yet.
To my dearest friend Simon, who on completion of this book has given me a paper shredder!

First published in 1999 by
New Holland Publishers (UK) Ltd
London · Cape Town · Sydney · Auckland

24 Nutford Place
London W1H 6DQ
United Kingdom

80 McKenzie Street
Cape Town 8001
South Africa

Level 1, Unit 4, 14 Aquatic Drive
Frenchs Forest, NSW 2086
Australia

10 9 8 7 6 5 4 3 2 1

ISBN 1 85974 073 1 HB

Editor: Melinda Coss
Editorial Assistant: Kate Latham
Design and Art Direction: Blackjacks
Photographer: Emma Peios
Managing Editor: Coral Walker

Reproduction by Modern Age Repro House Ltd, Hong Kong
Printed and bound in Singapore by Tien Wah Press (Pte) Ltd

Acknowledgements
The authors would like to applaud the following:
Yvonne McFarlane for the original score
Coral Walker for constructive chanting
Kate Latham for a fine chorus
Jack Buchan for design and orchestration
and a standing ovation to Emma Peios for her great photos.

Every effort has been made to present clear and accurate instructions. Therefore,
the author and publishers can offer no guarantee or accept any liability for any injury,
illness or damage which may inadvertently be caused to the user while
following these instructions.

contents

overt

I have been collecting and producing handmade paper for a very long time, being intrigued by the individuality, versatility and diversity of this seemingly ordinary, everyday product. I feel that we rarely spare the time to wonder how and where it evolved, nor do we think of the multitude of uses of this commodity called 'paper'. It can be thin and translucent, showing the fibres from which it was made, or, on the other hand, it can be tough, waterproofed, compressed and used commercially for making drums, cartons and parcel paper. Between these extremes are thousands of variations.

As you look through this book you will no doubt ask yourself why a paper making book follows a musical theme. I suppose that, in a similar way, I could just as easily have filled the book with references from literature. For where would we be without paper? Music could only ever be passed on by ear, stories only by word of mouth. Much would be lost forever.

Turn the paper pages of this book and you will be seeing – in a brand new light – the possibilities of making paper with flowers, grasses, vegetables and fibres, to say nothing of what you can do with all the ordinary paper that you undoubtedly possess. For those who are already keen paper makers, perhaps you will be like me and have boxes full of 'collectables' for use in that special piece of paper you hope to make one day.

Finally, do spare a wondrous thought for nature's paper maker, the wasp. The queen, who starts building her paper nest, mixes chewed wood pulp with saliva. In this fragile shell she makes the cells and lays the eggs for the first worker wasps who mature, and in their turn, continue to build a large paper house in which all the colony is raised. You will be pleased to know that the wasp's paper making method is not one which I advocate – but read on,

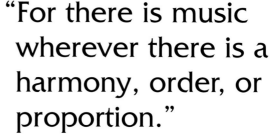

"For there is music wherever there is a harmony, order, or proportion."

Sir Thomas Browne (1605-1682)

and you will be surprised just how easy it is to produce your own beautiful and original papers.

I would personally like to thank Melinda Coss who has helped me write the pages of this book.

Angela Ramsay

ure

paper making
for the record

Throughout history many different materials have served the purpose of paper. Information has been recorded on clay, wood, metal, leaves and many other available resources. The engraving of a surface fulfils man's obsessive need to 'make his mark' on posterity.

In the beginning, around 4000 BC, the Sumerians communicated by means of 'pictographs', using clay tablets as a writing surface. By 3000 BC, these markings were refined into wedge-shaped (cuneiform) characters that were drawn with the edge of a sharp object.

Tree bark also provided a useful surface for recording notes. In many Pacific cultures, 'bark cloth' is made by beating sections of wet bark and joining them together with vegetable gums. Bark was also used by the people of Indonesia to record ideas on religion and magic. Coincidentally, Buddhists in India and south east Asia were busily inscribing the leaves of the bai-lan tree. These leaves were treated with sand, and marks were scratched into the leaf and then coloured with pigment. The leaves were then perforated and bound together to form books. (Which is why of course you are, at this moment, thumbing through the 'leaves' of this book.)

All cultures used the resources available to them to record information. For example, the ancient Chinese (who have never been short of rice) created what has become known as rice paper. This was, in fact, formed from the pith of the Fatsiapapyrifera plant and was so close to 'real' paper

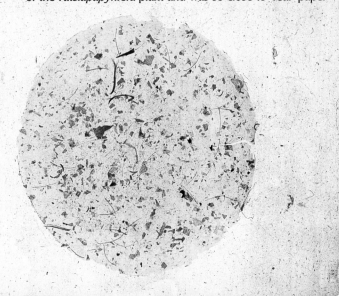

that even the English and Americans considered it good enough to import and use.

The word 'paper' itself derives from the papyrus plant, a reed which once grew in abundance along the banks of the Nile but is now found only in parts of Chad. The ancient Egyptians discovered that they could create a very stable writing surface from this plant. To make papyrus, the stalks of the plant were cut and peeled and the pith pounded into strips. A second layer of pith was applied on top and then the whole piece was beaten into a flat sheet and polished with an old bone.

FIBRE PAPER

It is, undoubtedly, the ancient Chinese who are credited with being the first 'real' paper makers. Widely recognised as probably the most important of these is Ts'ai Lun who, in 105 AD, announced his invention of paper to the Chinese Emperor. The basis of his recipe was hemp (used to make fishing nets) which he soaked and beat continuously with a wooden paddle to separate the fibres. This produced a porridge-like substance which was scooped up on to a mould in a similar manner to the method used by handmade paper makers today. The Chinese improved this technique by creating a bamboo cover for the surface of the mould. This smooth surface made it easier to free the paper and so increased the rate of production. The Chinese also discovered the value of starch as a sizing agent and incorporated a yellow dye in manuscript paper to repel insects.

It took around 500 years for the knowledge of paper making to reach Japan, and eventually on through Tibet and on to Central Asia. Here, in Samarkand, paper dates back to a battle in Turkestan where imprisoned Chinese artisans were forced to make the highly prized paper for their captors.

By the 8th century AD, paper making had spread westward through Baghdad to Egypt and Morocco, but it was not until the 10th century that the craft began to infiltrate Europe; although the Christians decided it was an unwelcome manifestation of Moslem culture. In 1221, the Holy Roman Emperor Frederick II went so far as to declare all documents written on paper invalid!

Attitudes changed in the 1400s when the first printing press was invented and things continued to improve with the pace of developing technology.

European paper makers used cotton and linen rags as the basis for their paper, soaking these in an alkaline solution before creating a pulp from the fibres and proceeding to form, press and dry sheets of paper using methods you are going to learn about in this book.

It wasn't until the 1700s that wood pulp became a viable option as the basis of paper. This was mainly owing to the work of Mathias Koops, who lived in England, and the increasing availability of mechanical wood grinders.

In the 1790s, American paper makers were experimenting with tree bark, sugarcane waste, straw and cornstalks, but it wasn't for another 70 years that the first US newspaper – the *Boston Weekly Journal* – was printed on paper made from ground-up wood.

In France in 1798, Nicholas-Louis Robert invented a prototype of a machine on which paper was formed on a continuous sheet of wire cloth. This was for the purpose of creating banknotes that were in very short supply following the French Revolution. The English patent for an improved version of the machine was secured by John Gamble in April 1801. This machine came to the attention of brothers Henry and Sealy Fourdrinier, who engaged engineer Bryan Donkin to build a new and further improved model. (Fifty years later, Donkin had designed 191 machines, mainly for Europe and Britain, but he did make two for the United States and one for India.)

In 1809, a cylinder-type paper machine was introduced by John Dickinson of Hertfordshire, England and, hot on his tail, Thomas Gilpin built the first cylinder machine in America.

While the industrial progress of paper making continues (and enables you to see this book in print), the 21st century heralds a healthy respect for environmental issues and, I hope, a continuing creative movement that will appreciate the artistry involved in producing paper by traditional methods.

the instruments

Many crafts rely heavily on the quality of equipment or instruments used in the process. Not so with paper making. One of its great advantages is that the equipment you don't already own can be improvised with various household items. The only unique tools are a deckle and mould and even these can be constructed very easily from a length of wood and some old net curtain (full instructions are given on page 11). If you don't have time to make one, a deckle and mould can be purchased from a craft shop or paper making supplier (see Stockists on page 79) where they are available in various sizes. Dig out the following items from your kitchen cupboard or garage and you will be ready to begin your paper making experience.

ABSORBENT KITCHEN CLOTHS: Used in the 'couching' process, see page 17.

BLENDER/LIQUIDIZER: For the purposes of paper making, a blender with a chamber is preferable to the 'stick' variety. If you don't already own one they can often be picked up very cheaply from garage sales. Although you can beat the paper to a pulp manually, using a blender saves an enormous amount of time and energy.

CLOTHES PEGS: These are used for hanging up wet sheets of paper to air-dry on an indoor washing line. Bulldog clips are a good alternative.

DECKLE AND MOULD: This is used to scoop up your pulp from the vat and to form neat sheets of paper. See the next page for full information.

ENAMEL OR STAINLESS STEEL SAUCEPAN: Used for boiling up plant fibres. Not required if you are simply going to recycle existing papers.

FUNNEL: For pouring the excess pulp into said jam jars/containers.

GRAVY BASTER: For dropping spots of pulp for decoration.

IRON: If you don't own one of these you are a person after my own heart. Relent and buy one if you want smooth paper that you can write on.

JAM JARS OR PLASTIC STORAGE CONTAINERS: For storing excess pulp.

MEASURING JUG: Used for measuring water to make pulp.

MESH SPLATTER COVER: This device (designed to prevent hot fat splashing from a frying pan) can be used instead of a deckle and mould. It enables you to make round sheets of paper.

NEWSPAPERS: While not useful as a paper making ingredient, newspaper is required for the 'couching' process. Couching is the method employed to create a stack or pile of sheets of paper, see page 17.

NYLON CURTAIN: This is especially handy if you intend making paper from silk tops. It can also be stretched over a frame to create a mould or can be used to drain away the water from excess pulp before storage.

PALETTE KNIFE: This is a useful tool for removing your paper from the mould. Either an artist's or kitchen knife will do the job. If you don't have either, use an ordinary sharp kitchen knife.

PLASTIC BUCKET: Required to soak your torn-up papers during the recycling process.

PLASTIC OR STAINLESS STEEL SPOON: Keep a selection of spoons for adding different coloured pulps and creative extras to your vat.

PRESS: This is used to press your wet paper and can be made from two pieces of laminated board and four G-clamps. Dry papers can be pressed under a pile of books or under any flat, weighted surface.

SHALLOW PLASTIC TRAY: This serves as a base for the couching process, see page 17.

SHEET OF GLASS: Used for creating a smooth writing surface on your paper. A mirror will do.

SPONGES: These are needed to mop up water spills and generally to keep your work surfaces and equipment spick and span.

VAT: See Washing Up Bowl below.

WASHING UP BOWL OR LARGE PLASTIC BOX: This is referred to throughout this book rather grandly as a 'vat'. It is the container you will use to hold your pulp and needs to be at least 4 in (10 cm) larger all round than your deckle and mould. If you choose to use a washing up bowl, use an oblong one. A cat litter tray is also ideal, but make sure you tell your cat first! For the enthusiast, it is worth buying several 'vats'.

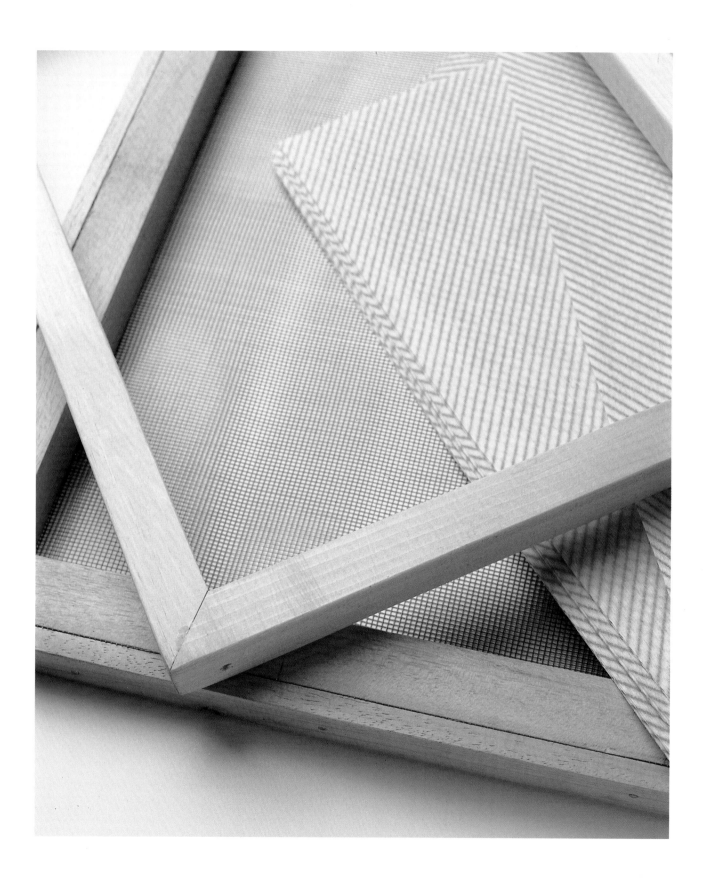

the deckle and mould

The deckle and mould are the prime pieces of equipment that transform your pulp into neatly formed sheets of paper. The size and shape of the mould dictate the size and shape of your paper. The deckle (from the German decke, meaning cover) is a frame that sits on top of the mould and holds the pulp in position during the 'scooping up' process. It is not essential to use a deckle but it does help to keep your paper to a uniform shape. The small amount of pulp that seeps between the edges of the deckle and mould creates a slightly wavy or 'deckle' edge which is a prized characteristic of handmade paper.

A mould can be constructed by covering a simple wooden frame with a taut mesh fabric, so forming a screen. The use of mesh enables the water to drain away from the thin layer of paper pulp that will settle on the surface of the screen and form the paper. A suitable mesh screen can be created using any of the following fabrics/materials:

❑ nylon curtaining
❑ silk screen mesh
❑ window screening
❑ plastic canvas (as used in cross stitch embroidery)
❑ mosquito netting

making a mould

To create a basic A4 (297 x 210 mm/11$\frac{3}{4}$ x 8$\frac{1}{4}$ in) frame you will need the following:

2 lengths of 40 x 5 x 2.5 cm (15$\frac{3}{4}$ x 2 x 1 in) pine
    or similar timber
2 lengths of 22 x 5 x 2.5 cm (8$\frac{1}{2}$ x 2 x 1 in) pine
    or similar timber
wood glue, hammer and nails or heavy duty staple gun
4 brass corner braces
polyurethane varnish

Lay the pieces of wood in an oblong with the two longer pieces outside the shorter pieces. (Note: the 5 cm (2 in) face should form the width of the timber and the 2.5 cm (1 in) face should form the depth). Glue the corners together with wood adhesive and nail them together through the outside edges of the timber. As an alternative, you can staple the joins together with a staple gun. Screw on the corner braces for further support. Coat all surfaces with polyurethane varnish to provide a waterproof finish. When the varnish is dry, dampen the mesh and stretch it over the surface of the mould until it is taut. Secure the mesh to the edges of the mould with staples.

making a deckle

Following the instructions above, make a second frame (without the mesh covering) to serve as a deckle. This should be made to exactly the same proportions as the mould. Both deckle and mould can be made to whatever size you wish but remember that your vat needs to be large enough to manoeuvre your hands, holding the deckle and mould together, in the pulp.

instant alternatives

t *here are several items that can be used very successfully as makeshift moulds and you may well already have these to hand. Here is a list of instant alternatives:*

Circular needlework frames: *these are available in numerous sizes and come with a tension screw attached. This will enable you to ensure that your mesh stays tightly stretched.*

Wooden stretchers: *used in both picture framing and as needlework frames, stretchers slot together into various sizes to form a solid frame. Secure your mesh to the edges with staples or tacks.*

Picture frame: *a ready-made picture frame will serve as a perfectly good mould once you have stretched and secured your mesh as described above.*

Mesh splatter cover: *offers yet another opportunity for making circular sheets of paper in various sizes.*

COMPOSING PAPERS

fortunately for the handmade paper maker one basic ingredient – waste paper – is readily available and commonly treated as trash. There is also something extremely rewarding about scavenging through waste paper baskets and transforming their contents into works of art. Alongside the basic pulp, you can have fun adding various colours and textures to your paper, as well as all manner of delicious items, such as leaves and petals, grasses, glitter and fruit peel. The great thing about paper making is that it is an inexpensive hobby. Any unsuccessful experiments on your part can be remedied swiftly and with little cost. However, for your guidance, here are the basic ground rules.

Sadly, not all paper products are suitable for recycling, so here is a list of waste products that you should keep for your paper making efforts and those you should discard.

PAPERS TO CHERISH
computer paper
shredded copy paper
tissue paper
crepe paper
art paper
thin card
egg boxes (the cardboard kind, not those made from polystyrene)
paper napkins
coloured envelopes
paper bags (brown and white)

PAPERS TO DISCARD
newspapers
glossy magazines and brochures
glossy or treated cardboard
heavily printed papers
papers marked with oil paints
thick card (takes far too long to soak, so not for the impatient enthusiast)

tap dance

The next ingredient to consider in the paper making process is water. In most areas tap water can be used without problems. However, if you are aware of impurities in your water supply you need to filter the water before use or they may surface and stain your finished paper. One preventative measure is to fix some gauze over the end of your water tap so that major impurities are filtered out. Alternatively (once you are an addicted paper maker), you may wish to consider using a water filter/purifier for this purpose.

The pH balance of your water can also affect the quality of your finished paper, as an excessive acid or alkaline content will, over time, cause discoloration and a brittle texture. Check the pH of your tap water with a tester (available from garden centres or shops selling aquarium equipment). The ideal pH for paper making measures in the region of 8 on the pH scale.

ACCOMPANIMENTS: Once you have your basic ingredients it is time to start thinking about additives for colour, scent and decoration. The recipes in this book will describe a number of techniques that you can use to incorporate additives but you may wish to chop and change the ingredients to create your own individual masterpieces.

adding colour

One of the easiest and most reliable ways to create coloured paper is to use coloured paper napkins as your basic pulp medium. These can be used on their own to produce bright colours or you can mix liquidized napkins with white pulp for pastel shades and speckled effects. Crêpe papers and coloured tissue paper can also be used for this purpose, although many brands are not colourfast and will dye not only the paper, but also any leaves, petals or decorative extras that are in the pulp.

Water-soluble textile dyes, such as Dylon, can be added to the pulp bath before you create your sheets of paper. Inks, water soluble powder paints and liquid food colouring are also useful dyeing agents. Add these during the blending process, in small amounts, until you achieve your desired effect. Your dry, finished paper will be several shades lighter than it appears in the wet pulp.

Natural dyestuffs offer a subtle range of colours, although these can tend to fade over time. Tea and coffee both produce reliable dyes and you should experiment with onion skins for golden and autumnal colourings, sloes and damsons for rich pink and plum shades. Boil these in a small amount of water to extract the dye. The depth of colour you achieve will depend on the quantity of vegetable matter you started with and the amount of liquid added to the bath. The colour of the basic paper pulp will also have a considerable effect on the colour of your finished paper.

❑ Many of the more adventurous natural dyes (as used in textile dyeing) require an acid mordant to prevent the colour from bleeding and to enable the dye to adhere to the fibre. The use of these dyes is therefore more complicated, so consult a serious dyer's manual before experimenting.

nature trail

Some of the most popular handmade papers rely on nature for their decorative elements. Fresh and dried flower petals, citrus peel, leaves, herbs and ferns, seed heads and grasses can all be included in your pulp bath or arranged in a formal design on your wet paper. However, fresh plants will release their own colour into the pulp so, before use, simmer the more rigorous plants, such as ferns, in boiling water for a few minutes and then lay them out on blotting or kitchen paper. If colour bleeds from the plants on to the paper, repeat the procedure.

Delicate petals should not be boiled but should be dried or pressed before use. If you own a microwave oven you can shortcut this process. Put leaves, petals or flowerheads on microwave kitchen paper and place in the microwave. Turn the control to high (100 per cent) and set for four minutes (three minutes for very delicate petals or flower heads).

high note

If you plan to write a personal letter on the paper you are making, design it according to the message you want to send. Here are some translations from the language of flowers and herbs which may help you make your choice of additives.

MESSAGE	FLOWER	MEANING
Get well soon	Balm of Gilead	Cure, relief
Poison pen letter	Basil	Hatred
Thank you note	White bell flower	Gratitude
	Flax	I feel your kindness
Moral support	Bluebell	Constancy
Warning	Borage	Bluntness
RSVP	Canterbury Bell	Acknowledgement
Well done	Fennel	Worthy of praise
Mother's Day	Moss	Maternal love
From the heart	Fern	Sincerity
Love letter	Forget me not	True love
	Honeysuckle	Love bond
Thinking of you	Pansy	Thinking of you
Letter to the boss	Sage	Esteem
Friendship	Ivy	Fidelity
I want a divorce	Oak	Bravery
You confuse me	Love in a mist	Perplexity
Offer of help	Mint	Virtue
In loving memory	Rosemary	Remembrance
Why haven't you written?	Thyme	Activity
Send money	Wheat stalk	Riches

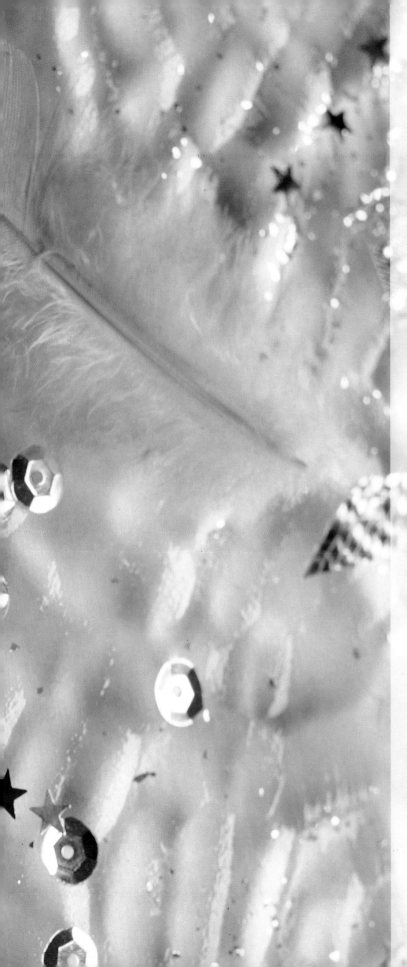

jazzy extras

If you are bored with political and ecological correctness, you can add all kinds of fun, zany elements to your pulp bath. Here is a list of possible inclusions for you to think about, but also experiment with other unusual items:

chopped up tinsel

glitter

scraps of satin ribbon

sequins

cut ends of threads

sawdust

coconut fibres

confetti

wool rovings (raw wool ready for spinning)

feathers

so scentsible

Having satisfied the sensual requirements of sight and touch, you may now wish to consider the delicious possibilities offered by scent. There are several simple ways of perfuming paper. The first is by adding dried, aromatic herbs to the pulp and the second is by adding a few drops of essential oil to the vat. Scented herbs or flowers, such as lavender, can be scattered in the pulp bath (where they will add texture in addition to scent) or they can be laminated on to the paper to form a motif or border design (see page 38). Herbs should be broken up into small leaf segments and dried (preferably in a microwave) before use. This will prevent the natural plant oils from staining your paper. Orange, lemon and lime zest or strongly scented flower petals (such as rose petals) will retain a mild scent once dried and they can be incorporated in the same way. Alternatively, scatter pot pourri into your pulp and enjoy an exotic mix of colour, texture and scent.

instant alternatives

a nother simple way of scenting your papers is to store them alongside a deliciously scented soap (one which is far too expensive to wash yourself with). You could also treat your paper to a light spray of your favourite perfume. For a truly heady experience, use a diffuser or atomiser to spray damp sheets of paper with essential oil. Refer back to High Note (opposite page) to decide which one to use.

jam session

With your major ingredients to hand, you are now ready to create your pulp. (See individual recipes for quantities.)

1 Tear your basic material into small pieces and soak it overnight in a bucket of cold water. Card needs to soak for 3 or 4 days. To hasten the process use hot water.

2 Put a handful of the soaked paper into a liquidizer and top up with water until it is three-quarters full.

3 Liquidize at a low speed for ten seconds. Repeat in ten second bursts until the paper is the consistency of thin porridge.

4 Empty the pulp into your vat and repeat these steps until all the waste paper is pulped.

5 Mix the pulp with cold water and scatter in any required additives now. Between the making of each sheet of paper, stir gently to distribute pulp and additives evenly.

6 Place the deckle on top of the mould and hold them vertically with the mesh facing you, dip them into the back of the vat, bringing them up into a horizontal position. Carefully lift the deckle and mould out of the pulp.

7 Shake gently to disperse the fibres evenly and then allow to drain for about 20 seconds. Tilt the mould slightly and drain for 10 seconds more.

8 Set down on a flat surface and carefully remove the deckle.

Congratulate yourself. You have just made your first sheet of paper.

storing pulp

i f you want to store your pulp it is best to do so before incorporating the additives. Let the pulp settle and drain off the excess water. You can then keep the pulp in the fridge in a sealed jar or plastic container for around two weeks. When you are ready to re-use it, place the pulp in nylon curtaining or cheesecloth and rinse it thoroughly with cold water before proceeding further. Pulp that has been coloured with vegetable matter should be stored in the freezer. Left to its own devices in the fridge the vegetable element may ferment and turn rancid if stored for more than a day or two.

couching

Once you have your first sheet of paper lying on the mould you have various choices to make regarding drying and pressing. If this piece of paper is intended as a one-off masterpiece you can leave it where it is to air dry and then gently ease it off the mould with a palette knife. Alternatively, if you want to make several sheets of paper from the pulp you will need to stack the papers up to dry. The stack is called a 'post' of papers and the method is known as 'couching'.

To couch a pile of papers you will need the following:
plastic tray
2 absorbent cloths for each sheet of paper
newspaper (tabloid size)
2 pressing boards
4 G-clamps or heavy weights
sponge for mopping up

Trim your cloths so that they are approximately 2 in (5 cm) larger than your mould.

MAKING A MOUND: Take two open sheets of newspaper and fold in half, then in half again, then in half again. Take two more open sheets of newspaper and fold in half twice. Lay them over the first sheets. Take two full sheets of newspaper and fold once. Place on top of the other papers. (This forms a mound in the middle of the paper.) Wet the stack of papers thoroughly.

Dampen one of the absorbent cloths and lay this on top of the newspapers, taking care to smooth out any wrinkles.

COUCHING: Removing the newly-made first sheet of paper from the mould by 'rolling' it on to the top of the cloth. For first-timers, you'll find the following method useful.

1 Hold the short ends of the mould and stand it on one long edge, positioning it in front of the couching mound with the paper facing the mound.

2 Tilt the mould towards the couching mound.

m ost of the recipes in this book make A5 sheets of paper. For those unfamiliar with this size, it measures 210 x 148 mm ($8\frac{1}{4}$ x $5\frac{3}{4}$in). This size is most commonly used for personal writing paper and, when folded in two, for notelets. Obviously, the size of your paper will depend upon your deckle and mould. A4 paper is twice the size of A5 and measures 297 x 210 mm ($11\frac{3}{4}$ x $8\frac{1}{4}$ in). A3 paper is twice the size of A4 and measures 420 x 297 mm ($16\frac{3}{4}$ x $11\frac{3}{4}$ in).

paper sizes

3 In one continuous movement, 'roll' the mould down firmly over the mound bringing the bottom edge of the mould up. At the same time, press the leading edge of the paper down on to the couching cloth. The paper should now be lying neatly on the couching mound.

Note: There should be no bubbles in the paper. If there are, place the pulp back into the vat and start again – practise makes perfect: do not be discouraged.

4 Dampen a second cloth and lay this on top of the paper. Dampen another cloth and add this to the pile.

5 'Roll out' a second sheet of paper from the mould and place on top of the first. Add another damp cloth. Continue in this fashion so that each sheet of paper is sandwiched between two cloths.

pressing and drying

Lift off no more than five paper 'sandwiches' (including cloths) and place these on your pressing board. Lay a piece of dry, folded newspaper on top of the pile.

Smooth out any wrinkles. Put the second pressing board on top of the papers and adjust G-clamps or add weights so that minimum pressure is applied. Leave for 10 minutes and then increase the pressure. Leave for a further 15 minutes then remove the post of papers and cloths from the press.

Once your papers come out of the press they are ready for drying. Remove each sandwiched paper separately with the cloths still in place and either lay out to dry on an absorbent surface (newspaper or old carpet will do nicely), or peg up the sandwiches on a clothes dryer or washing line. The latter option gives you the advantage of impressing your neighbours with your hard work. The most successful sheets of paper are those that are left to dry slowly. Do not dry them in hot sunlight or over a direct heat source.

When the paper is dry, iron it (inside the cloths) with the control set to cool or 'silk'. Carefully peel off the top and bottom cloths. If this presents any difficulty, slide a palette or sharp kitchen knife under a corner of the paper and carefully ease it away from the cloth. Once the papers are free, press them in the pages of a heavy book or between weighted boards for at least 24 hours.

sheet music —
creating a writing surface

If you intend to write on your paper it is important to create a smooth finish that will not absorb the ink. This can be done by 'sizing' the paper either during or after the paper making process. There are two methods.

USING SOAP AND STARCH SIZE: Take 1 tbsp of grated soap and dissolve it in boiling water. Add this to the vat together with 15 g (1 tbsp) of cold water starch dissolved in half a cup of cold water. Follow the general paper making instructions on page 16. Take papers and cloths from the press. Remove the cloth covering the face of the paper, placing the paper side down on to a laminated or glass sheet. Carefully smooth over the back of the cloth, pressing the paper edges down on the board or glass. Leave to air-dry for approximately 24 hours. When the paper is completely dry, ease off the remaining couching cloth, then – with a palette knife – remove the paper from the board or glass. Press the back of the paper with a cool iron. Stack the papers and place under a pile of books or weighted boards for a minimum of 24 hours.

USING GELATINE SIZE: This alternative method of sizing takes place after your paper is completely pressed and dry. To size five sheets of A5 paper, dissolve 1 tsp of powdered gelatine in half a cup of boiling water. Paint the gelatine solution over the surface of the paper with a soft, wide paintbrush (or spray it with a diffuser) and peg up the paper to air-dry. Once the surface is dry to the touch, add three cups of boiling water to the leftover gelatine solution and repeat the process. Hang the paper up to air-dry. If you wish to size both sides of the paper, repeat the process, painting the back once the front has dried.

'Sandwiches' of newly pressed papers can be air-dried on a clothes line. Do not rush the drying process: you will always achieve a more professional finish by letting nature take its course.

recycled

Some of the most exciting examples of handmade paper are made from recycling waste paper and lightweight card. This is done by reducing the material to a pulp, adding decorative extras and then re-constituting the pulp into sheets of paper. Not only is the method simple, but it also gives you the satisfaction of knowing that you are an ecologically sound and environmentally friendly person. In addition, you can give full rein to your creative talents by selecting additives to please and tease the imagination.

Not all paper products are suitable for recycling. Glossy magazines and brochures are coated with undesirable chemicals and are difficult to break down. Others contain colour or print that will bleed into the pulp. Excessive print will turn your paper an unattractive grey, so use clean, unprinted products whenever possible. In short, you will achieve your best results when using good quality, plain papers for recycling.

Once you have liquidized your pulp, you can add wild and brilliant colourings, exotic scents and interesting textures. You can then create thick and thin papers, wrapping papers and writing papers that carry your own personal hallmark.

papers

vivaldi:
the four seasons

This series of writing papers relies on seasonal gifts from nature for decorative effects. The variations in hue are created by using different coloured papers for each separate batch of pulp. Experiment with the wild flowers of spring and summer, or autumnal leaves. For winter, you could include traditional Christmas foliage, such as mistletoe or holly. The finished papers could be bound together to create a diary that reflects the season as you turn the pages. Alternatively, save flowers from that very special bouquet to create the pages of a memory book or wedding photo album.

spring

For a touch of spring, shade your paper using a basic pulp made from pale green, recycled paper. The careful pressing and drying technique described here ensures your paper will have a smooth writing surface.

❑ Makes four A5 sheets of one colour

approximately 40 g (1½ oz) of dry green
    coloured paper
green paper napkins
water
15 g (1 tbsp) grated soap dissolved in boiling water
15 g (1 tbsp) cold water starch dissolved in ½ cup
    of cold water
dried daisy, primrose, violet and forget-me-not
    flowers and petals

additional equipment
2 pressing boards 5 cm (2 in) larger than paper
4 G-clamps or heavy weights
laminated board or sheet of glass large enough
    to take four papers
couching cloths
newspaper
palette knife

Pulp paper as described on page 16, keeping the plain green paper (which will become the basic pulp) and the napkins (which will become the colourant) separate. Pour the basic pulp into the vat and add enough water to create the consistency of thin porridge. You'll need approximately 3 litres (5¼ pints). Now add the diluted soap and starch and stir gently.

Add a small amount of liquidized green paper napkin to this mixture and transfer one quarter of the mixture to another vat or storage container. Continue to add increasing quantities of green napkin mixture to the basic pulp, separating out a further quarter as the pulp becomes greener. Carry on in this way until you have four mixtures of pulp, each one a different shade of green. Then add dried daisy, primrose, violet and forget-me-not flowers and petals to the four vats of coloured pulp. Stir gently to avoid making air bubbles.

Holding the deckle and mould vertically with the mesh facing you, dip them in the back of the vat bringing them into a horizontal position. Holding them level, carefully lift the deckle and mould out of the pulp. Shake gently to disperse the fibres evenly, then allow to drain for about 20 seconds. Tilt the mould slightly and drain for 10 seconds more. Remove the deckle.

vivaldi: the four seasons

COUCHING: Prepare a mound of newspapers as described in full on page 17. Couch the paper on to the prepared mound. Cover with a second, damp couching cloth, taking care to smooth out any wrinkles. Place a third cloth smoothly on top of the second. Repeat this process for the second, third and fourth sheets of paper, positioning each sheet and covering the cloth directly above the one beneath, so building up a 'post' or stack of paper sandwiches.

PRESSING: Place the post on to a pressing board (see full instructions on page 18). Cover with a second pressing board and weight down with a heavy object or tighten screw clamps on your press. Leave the papers for ten minutes and then increase the pressure. Repeat every ten minutes for about half an hour to extract only the excess water.

SMOOTHING: Take the papers and cloths from the press. Remove the cloth covering the face of the paper and place it face down on a laminated board or glass sheet. Carefully smooth over the back and press the paper edges down on the board. Leave to air-dry for approximately 24 hours.

When the paper is completely dry, ease off the couching cloth, then, with a palette knife remove the paper from the board or glass. Press the back of the paper with an iron set at 'cool' or 'silk'. Stack the papers and place under a pile of books or boards and heavy weights for a minimum of 24 hours.

It isn't difficult to create these two-toned papers, but you will need two vats of different-coloured pulp. Dip one end of your mould into one colour, so that the pulp covers about half the surface area of your proposed paper sheet. Then turn the mould around and dip it into the other pulp, allowing the two colours to blend slightly as they meet.

summer

To represent summer I have used a basic pulp of different coloured papers and added calendula and sunflower petals, small sections of fern and summer grasses. The shaded effect was achieved by dipping two edges of the mould into two different coloured pulps.

vivaldi:
the four seasons

autumn

To give the papers a touch of autumn, the finely chopped skins of four red and four brown, medium-sized onions were boiled in separate pans for between 20-30 minutes. The liquid was then allowed to cool. A basic pulp was made from egg boxes. Each paper was made from the same vat with additional ingredients to create four slightly different finishes.

For paper 1 (below top), add a yoghurt pot full of pulped brown paper bags to the egg box pulp together with dried red autumn leaves.

For paper 2 (below centre) some brown onion water and skins were added to the pulp together with dried autumn bracken leaves.

Paper 3 (below bottom) uses additional brown paper pulp plus a yoghurt cup full of red and brown onion skins and a selection of small dried autumn leaves.

winter

To make the winter collection of Vivaldi papers, follow
the instructions above but replace the petals and ferns.
The paper above (top) is made using snowdrops dried
in the microwave (see Nature Trail on page 13). For the
second sheet, add small sprigs of fir dried in the
microwave before use. To create a really wintery effect,
a small amount of half liquidized silver tissue paper has
been added to the basic white pulp. The sheet here has
dried skeletons of holly leaves included in the pulp.
These leaves (from the previous season), were collected
from under a holly bush during the winter so they had
already lost their flesh. As an alternative, you can also
add tiny dried ivy leaves; the colour may bleed slightly
but the faded green edges contribute to the pretty
effect of trailing ivy.

punk rock

The driving force behind these papers was my desire to produce bright and vibrant colours. The papers you see opposite were produced from sheets of luminous poster paper. These papers are favoured by shopkeepers who use them to make display and 'sale' posters for their windows. Pop in just after the sale is over and see if you can beg some leftovers. Cut off any areas of heavy black ink before creating your pulp. The following instructions explain how to make different designs in one post of papers.

❏ Makes four A5 sheets of paper

equal amounts dry luminous poster paper in 4 colours
(approximately 40 g (1½ oz) in total)
water
15 g (1 tbsp) grated soap dissolved in boiling water
15 g (1 tbsp) cold water starch dissolved in ½ cup
of cold water

additional equipment
2 pressing boards 5 cm (2 in) larger than paper
4 G-clamps or heavy weights
couching cloths
newspaper
palette knife
small container (an old film canister is perfect)

Soak and pulp your paper as described on page 16, making each batch a separate colour.

MOTTLED, MULTI-COLOURED EFFECT: Place one quarter of each colour pulp into the vat and add enough water to create the consistency of thin porridge (approximately 3 litres [5¼ pints]). Now add the diluted soap and starch and stir gently. Holding the deckle and mould vertically with the mesh facing you, dip them in the back of the vat bringing them into a horizontal position. Holding them level, carefully lift the deckle and mould out of the pulp. Shake gently to disperse the fibres evenly, then allow to drain for about 20 seconds. Tilt the mould slightly and drain for 10 seconds more. Remove the deckle.

Couch the paper on to the prepared mound (see full instructions on page 17). Cover with two, damp couching cloths, taking care to smooth out any wrinkles.

DIAGONAL STRIPES: Take the small container and fill it with a single coloured pulp. Hold the mould above the vat and trickle the pulp diagonally across the corner. Repeat this process trickling separate colours of pulp across the mould, in diagonal lines, until it is covered. Couch the paper on to the cloth covering the mottled sheet of paper. Cover with two damp cloths. Smooth out any wrinkles.

HORIZONTAL STRIPES: Follow the instructions above for diagonal stripes, but trickle the separate bands of pulp horizontally across the mould.

HALF-AND-HALF: Select three colours of pulp and make a separate vat for each. Dip half the mould into the first colour then dip the other half of the mould into the second colour. Fill the container with the third contrasting colour and trickle the pulp, zig zag fashion, on to the mould where the first two colours join. Couch the paper on to the existing pile and cover with the last cloth. Smooth out any wrinkles.

Once you have completed your post of papers place it on to a pressing board (see full instructions on page 17). Cover with a second pressing board and weight it down with a heavy object or tighten the screw clamps on your press. Leave the papers for ten minutes and then increase the pressure. The pressing process is used to extract only the excess water. It should take about half an hour in total.

Remove the top pressing board. Now lift off the top cloth, paper and second cloth all together and peg up the paper sandwich on to a washing line or wire clothes hanger to dry. Separate the remaining papers in the same way and peg up alongside the first. When the papers are dry, iron them with the setting turned to 'silk', then carefully remove the papers from the couching cloths.

the blues

This paper gives you the perfect opportunity to shake off the blues. While making it you are officially allowed (probably for the first time in your life) to flick ink without getting into trouble! Splodge and blot to your heart's content to create this marvellously mottled paper.

❑ Makes four A5 sheets of one colour

approximately 40g (1½ oz) dry pale blue
    coloured paper
1 deep blue paper napkin
water
1 tbsp grated soap dissolved in boiling water
1 tbsp cold water starch dissolved in
    ½ cup of cold water
selection of shades of normal blue and
    black writing inks
small stick for flicking

additional equipment
2 pressing boards 5 cm (2 in) larger than paper
4 G-clamps or heavy weights
couching cloths
newspaper
palette knife

Pulp paper as described on page 16 and divide into four batches. Make a separate batch of pulp from the blue napkin. Place a batch of basic pulp into the vat and add enough water to create the consistency of thin porridge, approximately 3 litres (5¼ pints). Now add the diluted soap and starch and stir gently.

Holding the deckle and mould vertically with the mesh facing you, dip them in the back of the vat bringing them up into a horizontal position. Holding them level, carefully lift the deckle and mould out of the pulp. Shake gently to disperse the fibres evenly, then allow to drain for about 20 seconds. Tilt the mould slightly and drain again.

For paper 1 (opposite, bottom), trail blue ink across the surface of the very wet paper to form slightly feathered blobs. Remove the deckle then leave on the mould to dry. Carefully remove the paper with a palette knife.

Paper 2 (below) is made as above but add an egg cup full of liquidized napkin to the basic pulp. Leave the pulp on the mould to dry and then splatter with blue and black inks.

For paper 3 (opposite, top), more blue pulp has been added and blue-black ink splodged heavily over the surface of almost dry paper.

A mottled effect has been created on paper 4 (opposite, centre) by adding a small amount of white pulp to the existing dark blue used for paper 3. The ink has been watered down and trailed delicately over the paper when it was still very wet. When all the papers are dry and removed from the mould, press them between the pages of a heavy book for at least one week.

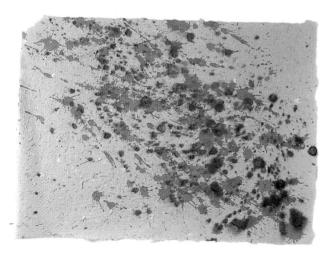

These papers are decorated at different stages of the drying process: the inks are added to paper 2 (left) when the paper is fully dry. Right, top to bottom: papers 3, 4 and 1.

*Pluck items from your sewing box to include in your papers such as threads, snippets of ribbon and scraps of
light fabrics. Bottom: paper 3, top, left to right: papers 2,1 and 4.*

chop-in prelude

So named because for these papers you 'chop' the additives and then add them 'in' to the pulp! These papers are perfect for greeting cards and notelets, and do remember that you can personalize them for individuals and special occasions by adding any of the additives and extras suggested on pages 14-15.

❑ Makes four A5 sheets of paper

approximately 40g (1½ oz) dry paper napkins in
    dark blue/purple, pale mauve and white
1 large sheet of blue/grey writing paper
water
15 g (1 tbsp) grated soap dissolved in boiling water
15 g (1 tbsp) cold water starch dissolved in ½ cup
    of cold water
scraps of ribbon, threads, tissue paper and organza

additional equipment
2 pressing boards 5 cm (2 in) larger than paper
4 G-clamps or heavy weights
couching cloths
newspaper
palette knife
pinking shears

Keeping the colours separate, pulp your paper and napkins as described on page 16. For paper 1 (opposite, top centre), place the darkest coloured pulp into the vat and add enough water to create the consistency of thin porridge. You'll need approximately 3 litres (5¼ pints). Now add the diluted soap and starch and stir gently. Sprinkle short ribbon cuttings into the mix and stir gently to avoid making air bubbles.

Holding the deckle and mould vertically with the mesh facing you, dip them in the back of the vat bringing them up into a horizontal position. Holding them level, carefully lift the deckle and mould out of the pulp. Shake gently to disperse the fibres evenly, then allow to drain for about 20 seconds. Tilt the mould slightly and drain for 10 seconds more. Remove the deckle, leave on the mould to dry, then remove carefully with a palette knife.

For paper 2 (opposite, top left), make your pulp from pale mauve paper napkins with a little white added. Follow the instructions for paper 1, but replace the short ribbon cuttings with longer pieces of ribbon or thread. (I used ones with a metallic thread running through them.) As you lift the mould from the vat, carefully trail some extra threads across the surface of the paper.

Paper 3 (opposite, main paper) is made from pale mauve and white napkin pulp plus a cup of blue/grey paper pulp. Cut scraps of organza with the pinking shears and add these to the pulp bath. Continue as for the original recipe.

Paper 4 (opposite, top right) is made with a mixture of mauve and white pulp to which a teaspoonful of purple pulp is added. Cut coloured tissue paper into shapes with pinking shears and float these in the pulp bath then continue as for the original recipe.

Any number of glittery bits can be added to the pulp: sequins, sparkly stars or little foil leaves.

rolling stones

These papers were made with mosses gathered from banks and from timber and stone. The background colours are soft, and creamy beiges make the paper look woody and natural. These papers use fresh moss, but dried moss works just as well, just omit the microwave stage.

❑ Makes four A5 sheets of paper

approximately 40g (1½ oz) white computer paper
A4 sheet of yellow/green paper
brown paper bag
water
15 g (1 tbsp) grated soap dissolved in boiling water
15 g (1 tbsp) cold water starch dissolved in ½ cup
    of cold water
assorted mosses

additional equipment
2 pressing boards 5 cm (2 in) larger than paper
4 G-clamps or heavy weights
laminated board or sheet of glass large enough
    to take four papers
couching cloths
newspaper
palette knife

Pulp the white, brown and yellow/green paper separately, as described on page 16.

Place the white pulp into the vat and add enough water to create the consistency of thin porridge, approximately 3 litres (5¼ pints). Now add the diluted soap and starch and stir gently. Microwave the mosses for 3 to 4 minutes at full power so they have a dry, crisp texture.

Sprinkle some moss into the white pulp and stir gently to avoid making air bubbles. Holding the deckle and mould vertically with the mesh facing you, dip them in the back of the vat bringing them up into a horizontal position. Holding them level, carefully lift the deckle and mould out of the pulp. Shake gently to disperse the fibres evenly, then allow to drain for about 20 seconds. Tilt the mould slightly and drain for 10 seconds more. Remove the deckle.

COUCHING: Couch the paper on to the prepared mound (see instructions on page 17). Cover with a second, damp couching cloth, taking care to smooth out any wrinkles. Place a third cloth smoothly on top of the second. Repeat the process for the second, third and fourth sheets of paper adding more coloured pulp and alternative mosses to each sheet. Position each sheet and covering cloth directly above the one beneath, so building up a 'post' of paper sandwiches.

PRESSING: Place the post on to a pressing board (full instructions appear on page 18). Cover with a second pressing board and weight down with a heavy object or tighten screw clamps on your press. Leave the papers for ten minutes and then increase the pressure. The pressing process is used to extract only the excess water. It should take approximately half an hour in total.

SMOOTHING: Take the papers and cloths from the press. Remove the cloth covering the face of the paper and place it side down on a laminated board or glass sheet. Remove the remaining cloth, smoothing over the back and pressing the paper edges down on the board. Leave to air dry for about 24 hours. When the paper is completely dry, ease off the couching cloth, then, with a palette knife, remove the paper from the board or glass. Press the back of the paper with a cool iron. Stack the papers and place under a pile of books for a minimum of 24 hours.

laminated

The word 'laminate' means to bond thin layers together and there are many reasons why a handmade paper maker should want to do this. Firstly, this technique gives you the opportunity to bond contrasting shapes on to your basic paper. Just think of the possibilities: plain papers can dance with polka dots, cut-outs of musical notes, fancy initials and you can create spectacular borders. All of these and many more interesting extras can become an integral part of your paper. Just use the simple methods on the following pages.

Laminating is also a technique used to protect a surface. By laminating paper with builders' scrim you can create a strong decorative fabric for individual items such as lampshades and book covers.

Of course, when you are bonding layers together you have the opportunity to sandwich decorative extras between these layers such as dried petals and leaves. This process protects fragile plants and gives you control over the finished designs.

By building up layers of pulp, you are thickening your paper into card and so adding to its durability. If you want a finer paper, thin your pulp with additional water.

With the exception of builders' scrim for three of the recipes, no additional materials or equipment are required for this technique.

papers

big bands

These papers show you the clever effects you can achieve by dipping your mould into contrasting coloured pulps. This technique enables you to create borders on your paper and, if you are feeling very creative, you can decorate the borders (and the papers) with dried flowers and leaves.

❏ Makes four A5 sheets of paper

approximately 40g (1½ oz) of white paper
rust-coloured paper napkins
water
15 g (1 tbsp) grated soap dissolved in boiling water
15 g (1 tbsp) cold water starch dissolved in ½ cup
    of cold water
dried flower petals and leaves

additional equipment
2 pressing boards 5 cm (2 in) larger than paper
4 G-clamps or heavy weights
laminated board or sheet of glass large enough
    to take four papers
couching cloths
newspaper
palette knife

Pulp the white paper and coloured napkins separately,
as described on page 16.

Place the white pulp into the vat with ½ cup of pulped
napkin. Add enough water to create the consistency of
thin porridge. You'll need approximately 3 litres (5¼ pints).
Now add the diluted soap and starch and stir gently.
Sprinkle some flower petals into the vat and stir gently to
avoid making air bubbles. Prepare a similar vat of plain
coloured pulp.

Holding the deckle and mould vertically with the mesh
facing you, dip the edges in the back of the coloured pulp
bringing them into a horizontal position. You now have a
band of pulp across the short end of the mould. Turn the
mould and repeat the process to create a band across one
long end of the mould. You should now have an 'L' shaped
border. Shake gently to disperse the fibres evenly, then
allow to drain for about 20 seconds. Tilt the mould slightly
and drain again. You can tidy the line by running a fine wet
paintbrush down the edge. Remove the deckle.

COUCHING: Couch the border on to the prepared mound
(see full instructions on page 17).

Now dip the deckle and mould into the pale-coloured
pulp and couch this on top of the coloured border.

Cover with a second, damp couching cloth taking care
to smooth out any wrinkles. Place a third cloth smoothly on
top of the second ready for the next paper.

PRESSING: Place the post on to a pressing board (see full
details on page 18). Cover with a second pressing board
and weight down with a heavy object or tighten screw
clamps on your press. Leave the papers for ten minutes and
then increase the pressure. The pressing process is used to
extract only the excess water. It should take approximately
half an hour in total.

SMOOTHING: Take the papers and cloths from the press.
Remove the cloths covering the faces of the papers, placing
the papers face down on a laminated board or glass sheet.
Carefully smooth over the back and press the paper edges
down on the board. Leave to air dry for approximately
24 hours. When the papers are completely dry, ease off the
couching cloth, then, with a palette knife, remove the
papers from the board or glass. Press the back of the paper
with a cool iron. Stack the papers and place under a pile of
books for a minimum of 24 hours.

variations

*For a slightly different effect, use the method
described above, but dip only two corners of your
deckle and mould into the coloured pulp. Couch these
on to the cloth covering the original paper. Now dip
the deckle and mould into the pale bath and, after
lifting them from the vat, remove the deckle and use
your finger to remove the corners of pale pulp from the
mould. Couch this sheet on top of the coloured corners
and cover with a damp couching cloth.*

*The paper with small leaves showing prominently on
the surface was made in the same way as the original
paper but the leaves were placed in position on the
cloth before the pale pulp was couched on to the
borders. When using this method, bear in mind
that your leaves or decorations will appear as a
reverse image. Cover the paper with a damp
couching cloth.*

dawn chorus

Builders' scrim is a wonderful addition to the paper maker's wardrobe. This fine netting is coated with a gluey substance that, when wet, adheres to a paper surface. This enables you to sandwich leaves and petals between paper and scrim so producing a highly decorative piece. Papers that are laminated with scrim are strong without being rigid. They are perfect for covering books and simple strips trimmed with pinking shears make decorative and long-lasting bookmarks.

❑ Makes four A5 sheets of paper

approximately 40 g (1½ oz) white crêpe paper
water
15 g (1 tbsp) grated soap dissolved in boiling water
15 g (1 tbsp) cold water starch dissolved in ½ cup cold water
dried marigold petals, ferns, pine needles, grasses
    and rose petals
builders' scrim

Pulp your paper as described on page 16. Place the pulp into the vat and add enough water to create the consistency of very thin porridge. You will need approximately 3 litres (5¼ pints). Now add the diluted soap and starch and stir gently.

Sprinkle a handful of dried grasses into the pulp. Holding the deckle and mould vertically with the mesh facing you, dip them in the back of the vat bringing them up into a horizontal position. Holding them level, carefully lift the deckle and mould out of the pulp. Shake gently to disperse the fibres evenly, then allow to drain for about 20 seconds. Tilt the mould slightly and drain for 10 seconds more. Leaving the paper on the mould, arrange some more dried grasses on the surface. Now lay strips of builders' scrim over the grasses until the paper is completely covered. Smooth over the scrim with your fingers and leave to air-dry on the frame.

When the paper is completely dry, ease it off the mould with a palette knife. Place the papers under a pile of books for a minimum of 24 hours.

variations

For variations in colours and textures — follow the instructions above, but replace the dried grasses with rose petals, fern leaves and pine needles or calendula petals.

polka

Here, contrasting polka dots have been laminated to circular paper which was made using an embroidery frame as a mould.

❏ Makes two 8 in circular sheets of laminated paper

approximately 40 g (1½ oz) contrasting coloured
　　paper napkins
2 sheets of black tissue paper
water
15 g (1 tbsp) per vat, of cold water starch (for the napkins
　　only) dissolved in ½ cup of cold water

additional equipment
embroidery frame
2 pressing boards 5 cm (2 in) larger than paper
4 G-clamps or heavy weights
couching cloths
newspaper
palette knife
gravy baster

Make up your separate coloured napkin pulps (mix the colours for shade variations) as described in the basic instructions on page 16, and – using a gravy baster – squeeze different sized drops of coloured pulp on to a mould and leave to air dry.

Place the black tissue paper pulp in the vat. Add enough water to create the consistency of very thin porridge. You'll need approximately 3 litres (5¼ pints).

Using a circular frame, dip it in the back of the vat bringing it up into a horizontal position. Holding it level, carefully lift it out of the pulp. Shake gently to disperse the fibres evenly, then allow to drain for about 20 seconds. Tilt the mould slightly and drain for 10 seconds more.

While still wet on the mould, arrange the dried paper circles in a pattern on to the surface of the paper. Leave on the mould to air dry, then remove and press with a cool iron. Stack the papers and place them under a pile of books for a minimum of 24 hours.

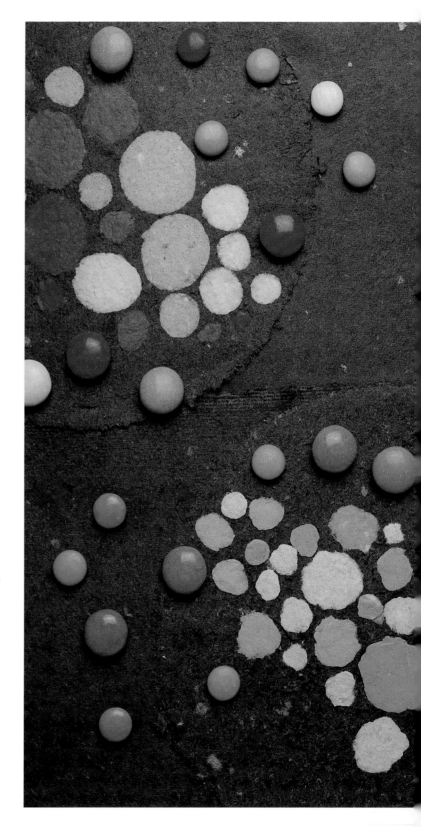

christmas carols

With all this expertise under your belt you can now enchant your friends with a range of beautiful handmade Christmas cards. I have used feathers, glitter and sequin stars to decorate the cards but you might also consider using tinsel or mistletoe as a basis for your design.

❑ Makes two laminated cards

approximately 80 g (3 oz) of paper: I used printers' red waste, red paper napkins, red crêpe paper, silver tissue paper, white recycled envelopes
water
15 g (1 tbsp) per vat of cold water starch dissolved in $\frac{1}{2}$ cup of cold water

additional equipment
2 pressing boards 5 cm (2 in) larger than paper
4 G-clamps or heavy weights
couching cloths
newspaper
palette knife
builders' scrim
glitter and sequin stars

Make up the coloured pulps, as described in the basic instructions on page 16.

Place the white pulp into the vat with a tablespoonful of silver pulp. Add enough water to create the consistency of very thin porridge. You'll need approximately 3 litres (5$\frac{1}{4}$ pints). Now add the starch and stir gently. Holding the deckle and mould vertically with the mesh facing you, dip them in the back of the pulp vat bringing them up into a horizontal position. Holding them level, carefully lift them out of the pulp. Shake gently to disperse the fibres evenly, then allow to drain for about 20 seconds. Tilt the mould slightly and drain for 10 seconds more. Remove the deckle.

COUCHING: Couch the paper on to the prepared mound (see full instructions on page 17). Cover with builders' scrim then couch a second piece of white paper on to the scrim, sprinkle with glitter and sequin stars. Cover with a second damp couching cloth taking care to smooth out any wrinkles.

PRESSING: Place the paper and cloths on a pressing board (see full instructions on page 18). Cover with a second pressing board and weight down. Leave the papers for ten minutes and then increase the pressure. The pressing process should take approximately half an hour in total.

SMOOTHING: Remove the top pressing board and carefully peel away the papers still attached to their cloths. Leave to air dry. Press the back of the paper with a cool iron. Place under a pile of books for a minimum of 24 hours. Fold the card by running the back of a craft knife along the crease.

variation

*f*ollowing the above method, add some glitter to the red vat then make and couch one red sheet of paper. Now make another sheet dipping the short edge of the mould into red pulp and the long edge into white pulp. Allow the colours to blend on the mould. Couch this on top of the existing red sheet of paper. Lay a few sequin stars on the surface and continue by pressing and drying.

opening night

This paper demonstrates how you can laminate all kinds of decorative features and extras on to your paper. Here, I have created the ultimate Christmas wrapping paper, complete with handmade ties to add a spectacular finishing touch.

❑ Makes one A3 and one A4 sheet of laminated paper
   plus three ties

approximately 120 g (4½ oz) of paper: red printers' waste,
   paper napkins and tissue paper plus a small quantity
   of gold tissue paper
water
15 g (1 tbsp) grated soap dissolved in boiling water
15 g (1 tbsp) cold water starch dissolved in ½ cup
   of cold water

additional equipment:
A4 and A3 sizes of deckle and mould
couching cloths
newspaper
palette knife
strips of gold net
builders' scrim
narrow satin ribbon
gold glitter
sequin stars

the paper

Make up the coloured pulp by finely liquidizing the printers' waste and coarsely liquidizing the tissue and napkins. Place the pulp into the vat. Add enough water to create the consistency of very thin porridge. You will need approximately 4 litres (7 pints). Now add the starch and stir gently.

   Make one A4 sheet first. Holding the deckle and mould vertically with the mesh facing you, dip them in the back of the pulp vat bringing them up into a horizontal position. Holding them level, carefully lift them out of the pulp. Shake gently to disperse the fibres evenly, then allow to drain for about 20 seconds. Tilt the mould slightly and drain for 10 seconds more. Remove the deckle. While the paper

is still on the mould sprinkle gold net cuttings on to the surface, gently press them into the pulp with your fingertips. Leave to air-dry then remove from the mould.

   Now make an A3 sheet from the same pulp. While the paper is still on the mould, lay four strips of netting down the length of the paper. Place the dry A4 sheet on top of the netting and across the centre of the paper. Leave on the mould to air-dry. When dry, remove from the mould, cover the back of the paper with a cloth and iron with the temperature set at 'silk'.

gift ties

Make one A4 sheet of red paper as described above. While the paper is still wet on the mould, evenly space a row each of glitter, stars and a double row of ribbon down the length of the paper (Note: allow the ribbons to overlap at each end to form ties).

   Now lay strips of builders' scrim over the surface of each decorated row. Leave to air-dry. Remove from the mould and trim into three separate bands.

pastoral symphony

An undulating landscape and seascape provide the themes for this heavily textured paper.
Here you will learn some clever tricks of the trade such as how to create shapes and lines in
different colours on a single sheet of paper.

❏ Makes two A4 sheets of laminated paper

approximately 160 g (6 oz) of paper: white computer
    paper and printers' waste, varying shades of blue
    and green napkins and tissue paper, small quantity of
    orange/yellow napkins

water

additional equipment
laminated board
palette knife
empty container (eg a yoghurt pot)
medium-sized artist's paintbrush

seascape

Make up a batch of white pulp (following the instructions on page 16) and separate batches of pulp for each shade of blue and the orange/yellow. Place the darkest blue pulp in the vat. Add enough water to create the consistency of very thin porridge.

Scoop up some dark blue pulp into the container and pour it, in a wavy line, across the top of a long edge of the mould. Add some lighter blue pulp to the vat and stir gently. Make another similar line under the first. Make two more lines adding lighter pulp for each line. (Note: do not be concerned if the lines intermingle.) Leave to air-dry, then remove carefully from the mould and lay the paper on the board.

Using a wet paintbrush, moisten the defining lines between the shaded blue 'waves' and carefully pull each wave apart from the one above it. Now make a sheet of paper from white pulp and, while it is wet on the mould, lay the darkest blue wave back into position on the surface of the white paper. Dribble a small quantity of orange/yellow pulp above the dark blue line to form a sunset effect. Lay the remaining 'waves' into position, leaving a fine band of white showing through between each wave. Leave to dry on the mould.

landscape

Repeat the process as above but using shades of green instead of blue to create a rolling, verdant landscape.

papers from

Paper made from fruit and vegetables is
gloriously strange. The natural colourings
become almost translucent and the texture is like
fine, plasticized card although, make no mistake,
this is frail stuff and it can be brittle. This fragility
is reduced by the addition of soap. For the creative soul, much will
depend on your choice of vegetable: cut a selection into fine slices and
take a close look at the shapes and patterns. Exotic fruits, such as star fruit
and kiwi, offer extraordinary possibilities, while the humble beetroot and
carrot have fascinating cross-section patterning. Consider also the
possibilities of pineapple, parsnip, celery, aubergine and courgette - the
list is virtually endless.

There are various methods for creating papers from fruit and vegetables.
The first is a laying and pressing technique for which you will need fine
cotton or calico cloth in addition to your basic equipment. When using this
method, the cellulose matter in the selected vegetables ensures that the
slices adhere to each other to form flat sheets of paper. The second method
is to create a pulp which releases the cellulose matter and then to recycle
the pulp in the normal way. This is the technique used for the cornhusks
paper (see page 53).

Once you have experienced the results of these papers, you'll be busy
for hours experimenting with the contents of your vegetable rack and
fruit bowl.

fruit

&

vegetables

take your cue!

It is hard to believe that this watery vegetable can produce such a beautifully delicate paper. If you don't have a cucumber to hand, try using marrow or courgette; the final results are very similar. Alternatively, this is the method you should use for kiwi, star and citrus fruit.

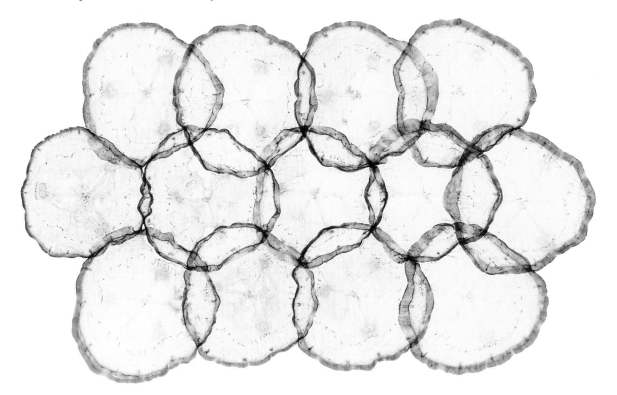

1 medium-sized, firm cucumber
sharp serrated knife
2 pressing boards 5 cm (2 in) larger than paper
4 G-clamps or heavy weights
calico or fine cotton cloths
newspapers
acid-free tissue paper

Place several sheets of newspaper on a pressing board and cover with a piece of calico. Cut the cucumber (with skin intact) into approximately 5 mm ($\frac{1}{4}$ in) thick slices and arrange these on the calico, making sure that the slices overlap. Cover with a second piece of calico and place several sheets of newspaper on top.

PRESSING: Put the second pressing board on top and adjust clamps to press gently for two hours. Increase the pressure and leave for another two hours. Open the press and replace the newspapers (which will now be damp). Press at full pressure for another four hours then replace the newspapers again.

Keeping the pressure at full, change the newspapers morning and evening for the next two days then once a day for the following four days. Remove the paper from the press (making sure that it is completely dry), very carefully peel the paper off the calico and store it in acid-free tissue paper.

Displayed between two sheets of glass with light shining from behind, this spectacular paper has all the translucent qualities of pale stained glass.

welsh choir

I think this should be considered the national paper of Wales. It has the texture of papyrus and makes use of the fine, long leaves of the leek. Select really long, straight leeks to achieve a successful finish. And because of the 'warp and weft' design, you end up with a great two-tone effect.

2 medium, straight leeks
sharp, serrated knife
2 pressing boards 5 cm (2 in) larger than paper
4 G-clamps or heavy weights
calico or fine cotton cloths
newspapers
acid-free tissue paper
saucepan

Cut off the top and bottom of the leeks and blanch the remaining parts in boiling water for five minutes. Remove from the pan and allow to cool.

PRESSING: Place several sheets of newspaper on the pressing board and cover with a piece of calico. Slit each

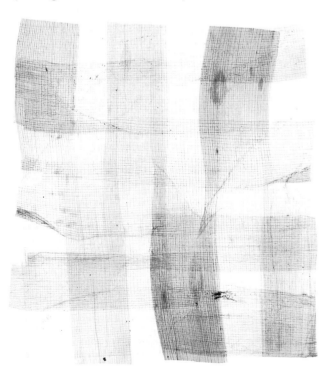

leek leaf separately from the top 'V' downwards. Place a vertical layer of leaves on the calico (slippery side up) making sure that they overlap and positioning them alternately so the greenish top end of one lies next to the white bottom end of the next. Now, working in the same way, place a horizontal layer of leaves on top (slimy side down) so the two layers will adhere. Cover with a second piece of calico and place several sheets of newspaper on top. Put the second pressing board on top and adjust clamps to press gently for two hours. Increase the pressure and leave for another two hours. Open the press and replace the newspapers (which will now be damp). Press at full pressure for another four hours then replace the newspapers again. Keeping the pressure at full, change the newspapers morning and evening for the next two days then once a day for the following four days. Remove the paper from the press (it should now be completely dry) and store it in acid-free tissue paper.

beet-hoven's symphony

This is the paper that Beethoven would have created had he chosen to compose paper rather than music! The glorious colour of cooked beetroot is put to good use in this exciting paper. Display it between glass sheets with back lighting to get the full, stained-glass effect.

4 small uncooked beetroots
sharp, serrated knife
2 pressing boards 5 cm (2 in) larger than paper
4 G-clamps or heavy weights
calico or fine cotton cloths
newspapers
acid-free tissue paper
saucepan

Cook the unpeeled beetroot in boiling water until they are just soft enough to put your fingernail into (approximately 10 to 15 minutes). Remove from the pan and cut into 5 mm ($\frac{1}{4}$ in) thick slices.

PRESSING: Place several sheets of newspaper on the pressing board and cover with a piece of calico. Arrange the beetroot slices on the calico, making sure that they overlap. Cover with a second piece of calico and place several sheets of newspaper on top. Put the second pressing board over the newspaper and adjust clamps to press gently for two hours. Increase the pressure and leave for another two hours. Open the press and replace the newspapers (which will now be damp). Press at full pressure for another four hours then replace the newspapers again. Keeping the pressure at full, change the newspapers morning and evening for the next two days then once a day for the following four days. Continue until fully dry. Remove the paper from the press, gently peel the paper from the calico and store it in acid-free tissue paper.

carrot paper

This is made in exactly the same way as the beetroot paper. Top and tail the carrots and then blanch them in boiling water for six to eight minutes. Let them cool, then cut them into 5 mm ($\frac{1}{4}$ in) thick slices before laying them on the calico. This method can also be used for parsnips, aubergines and celeriac, provided you adjust the cooking time.

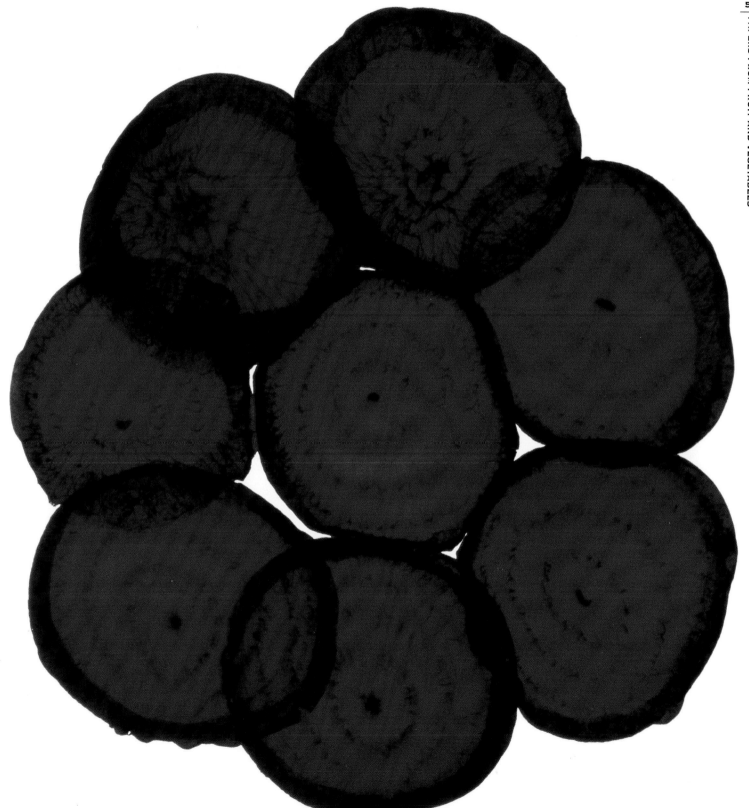

cornetto

For this recipe, you need cornhusks, but this doesn't mean you need to eat corn on the cob every night. Most supermarkets and greengrocers strip off the outer husks before displaying their corn, so all you have to do is ask nicely and they may give you a large bag free. Another option is to hang around street markets just as they are about to close. You'll find all sorts of recyclable treasures, including corn husks!

❑ Makes two A4 sheets of paper

approximately 60 g (2¼ oz) of dried corn husks
water
3 tbsp grated soap dissolved in boiling water
2 tbsp soda ash (sodium carbonate) or 3 tbsp washing soda

additional equipment
2 pressing boards 5 cm (2 in) larger than paper
4 G-clamps or heavy weights
net bag (made from nylon curtaining) or nylon stocking
newspaper
palette knife

Chop up the corn husks and boil them in water with the soda ash or soda for three hours, leave to cool. Drain into a net bag and rinse thoroughly, squeezing the bag continuously until the water runs clear. Place in the blender with water and liquidize until approximately half the fibres are broken up. Pour the pulp into your vat then add the water and the diluted soap. Stir gently.

Holding the deckle and mould vertically with the mesh facing you, dip them in the back of the vat bringing them up into a horizontal position. Holding them level, carefully lift the deckle and mould out of the pulp. Shake gently to disperse the fibres evenly, then allow to drain for about 20 seconds. Tilt the mould slightly and drain for 10 seconds more. Remove the deckle.

COUCHING: To create a smooth paper, couch the paper on to the prepared mound (see full instructions on page 17). Cover with a couching cloth.

PRESSING: Place the post on a pressing board 5 cm (2 in) larger than the finished size of the papers (see full instructions on page 18). Cover with a second pressing board and weight down with a heavy object or tighten G-clamps on your press. Leave the papers for ten minutes and then increase the pressure. The pressing process is used to extract only the excess water. It should take approximately half an hour in total.

SMOOTHING: Lift off the top pressing board and remove the paper with the top and bottom cloths still attached. Peg up to air dry. When the paper is completely dry, press the back with an iron set at 'silk' to produce a smooth surface. Place under a pile of books for a minimum of 24 hours.

For a more textured effect, do not press but leave the pulp to air-dry on the mould.

banana
boat song

☐ Makes two A4 sheets of paper

6 whole, medium sized bananas
water
3 tbsp grated soap dissolved in boiling water

additional equipment
2 pressing boards 5 cm (2 in) larger than paper
4 G-clamps or heavy weights
circular embroidery frame
nylon curtaining (to cover frame)
newspaper
palette knife

variation

Whilst pure banana pulp creates a decorative paper, more practical results can be achieved by liquidizing just the banana skin and adding it to a pulp made from plain white paper. Couch, press and iron your paper in the normal way.

Cut each banana lengthways and then three times across (making eight pieces). Boil them in water for half an hour, leave to cool. Place in blender and liquidize to the consistency of thin porridge (adding more water if required). Pour the pulp into your vat. Add diluted soap and stir gently.

Holding the frame with the mesh facing you, dip it in the back of the vat bringing it up into a horizontal position. Holding the frame level, carefully lift it out of the pulp. Shake gently to disperse the fibres evenly, then allow to drain for about 20 seconds. Tilt the frame slightly and drain for 10 seconds more. Couch the paper on to the prepared mound (see instructions on page 17).

Cover with a couching cloth and leave to air-dry very slowly in a well ventilated space. When the paper is completely dry, press the back with an iron set at 'silk'. Place under a pile of books for a minimum of 24 hours. The paper, opposite, was made in a similar way using a thicker pulp and a deckle and mould.

laid fibre

It is debatable whether these stunning creations should, in fact, be called paper rather than fabric, but since the technique produces firm, flat sheets with all the qualities of paper, I beg artistic licence here. Laid fibre papers are quick and simple to make and, like pulp papers, they can be designed to be as fine as lace or as thick as a medium-weight fabric. For embroiderers, the thicker papers offer the opportunity of creating a unique background fabric; for the artist, laid fibre paper is the perfect collage medium. It is also possible to mould wet fibre papers into free-standing shapes so even sculptors will find a use for this material.

Laid fibre papers are generally made from 'tops' which are available from weaving suppliers or textile mills in a good variety of colours and textures. A 'top' is a large sliver of parallel fibres produced after the carding and combing process but before spinning. Tops produced from natural fibres are pulled from the length of the top, while those made from synthetics sometimes require cutting with scissors. If you have a special shade in mind you can dye tops with natural or chemical dyes. Patterns can be built into your paper by arranging small pieces of coloured top on a contrasting background. Alternatively, your finished paper can be hand-tinted with textile paints to create a water-coloured effect.

Fibre papers are generally very delicate. For a stronger paper, use diluted half and half PVA glue with water instead of wallpaper paste. To give the papers even more substance, you can add extra layers of fibres, taking care to place each new layer in the opposite direction to the one beneath.

papers

rhapsody in silk

Luxurious silk 'papers' are surprisingly easy to make and have many decorative uses. Their wonderful sheen provides the perfect backdrop for creative embroidery and they are popularly used within collages. The finished 'paper' is very delicate but it can be backed with an iron-on interface which will add strength.

❏ Makes one A3 sheet of paper

2 pieces of net slightly larger than A3 size
30 g (1⅛ oz) white silk tops
small amount of coloured silk tops for decoration
wallpaper paste dissolved in water as per
    manufacturer's instructions
few drops of washing up liquid in 250 ml (½ pint) of water

additional equipment
plastic sheet to protect table
5 cm (2 in) paintbrush
newspaper
sponge

Place one piece of the net on your work surface. Pull off a length of the white silk top (approximately 20 cm [8 in]) and divide lengthways into manageable strips. Starting at one end of the net, hold down the end of a strip of silk top on to the surface of the net. Pull the main strip away leaving the held down fibres on the net. Repeat this process, laying the fibres in one direction only, until the net is completely covered. Working in the same direction, add another layer if required. Note: the thickness of the layer of fibres will determine the thickness of the finished paper.

Now, arrange your coloured top fibres on the surface for decoration. Carefully place the second piece of net over the laid silk top.

WETTING THE SILK: Taking care not to disturb the laid fibres, paint them over with the washing up liquid solution using a 5 cm (2 in) paintbrush. Carefully lift the two layers of netting and turn the silk over. Wet the underside in the same way. Mop up any excess water with a sponge.

Now repeat the process, but this time paint the top and underside of the silk with the wallpaper paste. Dry flat on a piece of dry newspaper then peel off the top net. When dry, remove the bottom net. Press over a cloth with a cool iron.

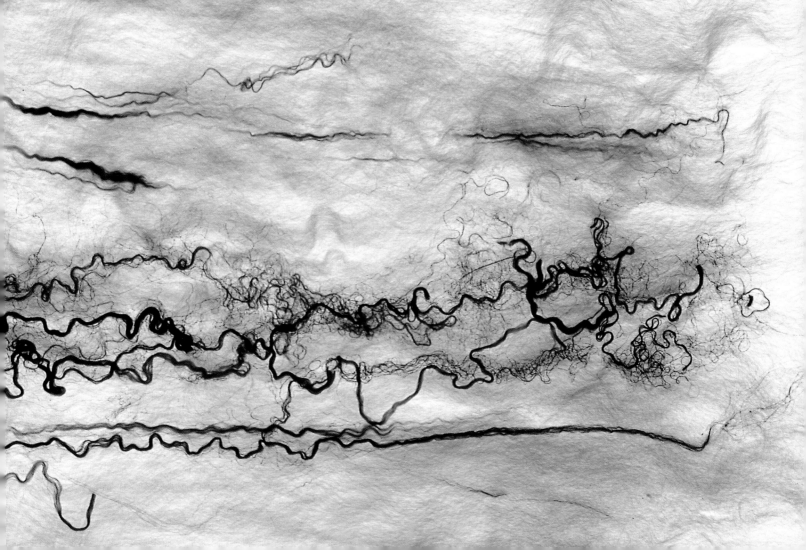

water music

❏ Makes one A3 sheet of paper

2 pieces of net slightly larger than A3 size
30 g ($1\frac{1}{8}$ oz) white silk tops
piece of lightweight silk wadding the size of finished paper
pot pourri flowers
small amount of coloured silk tops to match the colour of the
    pot pourri flowers
wallpaper paste dissolved in water as per
    manufacturer's instructions
few drops of washing up liquid in 250 ml ($\frac{1}{2}$ pt) water

additional equipment
plastic sheet to protect table
5 cm (2 in) paintbrush
newspaper
sponge

Place one piece of the net on your work surface. Cover with the silk wadding. Pull off a length of the silk top (approximately 20 cm/8 in) and divide lengthways into manageable strips. Hold down the end of a strip of silk top on to the surface of the wadding, pull the main strip away leaving the held down fibres on the net. Repeat this process, laying the fibres in one direction only, until the wadding is sparsely covered. Now, arrange your pot pourri flowers with a few coloured top fibres on the surface for decoration. Carefully place the second piece of net over the top.

WETTING THE SILK: Taking care not to disturb the arrangement, use the brush to paint the surface of the net with the washing up liquid solution. Carefully lift the two layers of netting and turn the silk over. Wet the underside of the wadding in the same way. Mop up any excess water with a sponge.

Now repeat the process, but this time paint the surface and underside of the silk with the wallpaper paste. Place flat on a piece of dry newspaper then carefully peel off the top net. When dry, remove bottom net. Press over a cloth with the iron set to 'cool' or 'silk'.

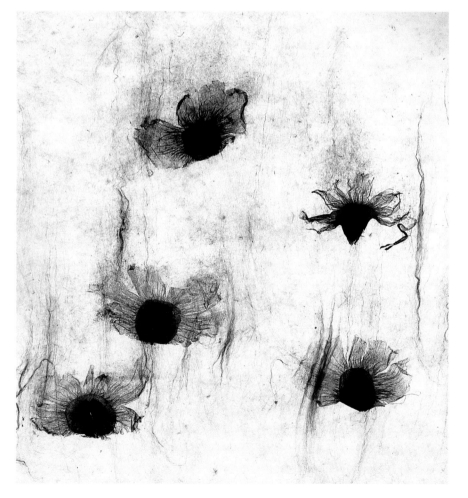

textile **trio**

Apart from silk, other fibres can be used most successfully to make paper. Made in a similar way to silk papers, these 'textile' papers resemble fabric, but can be treated like paper. They are perfect for decoration and make the most marvellous pieces for collage and artwork.

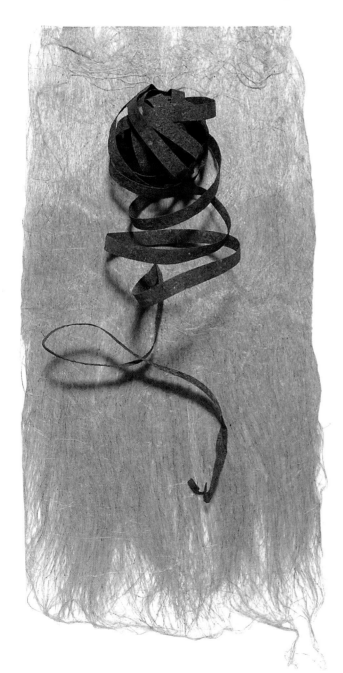

flax

Flax (from the plant *Linum*) is the fibre that is used to create linen. Paper was traditionally created by boiling linen (or cotton) rags in an alkaline solution. The softened fibres were then beaten and bleached before the paper was formed. For our purposes, I have laid the raw flax fibre tops to produce a decorative textured paper.

❑ Makes two A4 sheets of paper

2 pieces of net slightly larger than A4 size
30 g (1⅛ oz) flax tops
wallpaper paste dissolved in water as per
    manufacturer's instructions
few drops of washing up liquid in 250 ml (½ pint) of water

additional equipment
plastic sheet to protect table
5 cm (2 in) paintbrush
newspaper
sponge

Place one piece of the net on your work surface. Pull off a length of the flax top (approximately 20 cm [8 in]) and divide lengthways into manageable strips. Hold down the end of a strip of flax top on to the surface of the net, starting at the right-hand end. Pull the main strip away leaving the held down fibres on the net.

Repeat this process, laying the fibres in one direction only until the net is completely covered. Working in the same direction, add another layer, if required. Note: the thickness of the layer of fibres will determine the thickness of the finished paper. Carefully place the second piece of net over the laid flax top.

WETTING THE FLAX: Taking care not to disturb the laid fibres, paint them over with the washing up liquid solution using a 5 cm (2 in) paintbrush. Carefully lift the two layers of netting and turn the flax over. Wet the underside in the same way. Mop up any excess water with a sponge.

Now repeat the process but this time paint the top and underside of the flax with the wallpaper paste. Dry flat on a piece of dry newspaper then carefully peel off the top net. When dry, remove bottom net. Press over a cloth with the iron set to 'silk'.

mohair

Unfortunately, no one has yet discovered a live 'mo'. Its fibres, however, live on that angelic creature the angora goat, named after the region in Turkey where it was first reared. Mohair tops are available in a wide range of plain and variegated colours. This is a surprisingly sturdy fibre, given its delicately lustrous appearance.

❏ Makes one A3 sheet of paper

2 pieces of net slightly larger than A3 size
30 g (1⅛ oz) mohair tops in greens, reds and blues
wallpaper paste dissolved in water, as per manufacturer's
    instructions
few drops of washing up liquid in 250 ml (½ pint) of water

additional equipment
plastic sheet to protect table
5 cm (2 in) paintbrush
newspaper
sponge

Place one piece of the net on your work surface. Pull off lengths of coloured mohair top (approximately 20 cm [8 in]) and divide lengthways into manageable strips. Hold down the end of a strip of mohair top on to the surface of the net, pull the main strip away, leaving the held down fibres on the net.

Repeat this process, alternating the colours and laying the fibres in one direction only, until the net is completely covered. Carefully place the second piece of net over the laid mohair tops.

WETTING THE MOHAIR: Taking care not to disturb the laid fibres, paint over them with the washing up liquid solution using a 5 cm (2 in) paintbrush. Carefully lift the two layers of netting and turn the mohair over. Wet the underside in the same way. Mop up any excess water with a sponge.

Now repeat the process but this time paint the top and underside of the mohair with the wallpaper paste. Dry flat on a piece of dry newspaper then carefully peel off the top net. When dry, remove bottom net. Press over a cloth with the iron set to 'silk'.

viscose

These fibres are used in the manufacture of rayon and viscose. While they are manmade as opposed to natural, they offer interesting possibilities to the paper maker because of their strength. Viscose fibres are very lustrous and can be cut and manipulated into curls for decorative collages. The tops tend to be continuous and can be cut into manageable lengths with scissors before use. Viscose takes colourings extremely well and this is an excellent opportunity to experiment with fabric dyes.

❏ Makes one A3 sheet of paper

2 pieces of net slightly larger
    than A3 size
30 g (1⅛ oz) of viscose tops
wallpaper paste dissolved in
    water as per manu-
    facturer's instructions
few drops of washing up liquid
    in ¼ litre (½ pint) of water

—tip

try experimenting with ordinary bathroom cotton wool. Using the method described above you can work with virtually any fibre.

additional equipment
plastic sheet to protect table
5 cm (2 in) paintbrush
newspaper
sponge

For curly viscose paper, cut short lengths of viscose, and arrange them randomly on the surface of the net pulling them apart into curls. Make sure the net is completely covered. Carefully place the second piece of net over the laid viscose tops.

WETTING THE VISCOSE: Taking care not to disturb the laid fibres, use the paintbrush to paint over them with the washing up liquid solution. Carefully lift the two layers of netting and turn the viscose over. Wet the underside in the same way. Mop up any excess water with a sponge.

Now repeat the process but this time paint the top and underside of the viscose with the wallpaper paste. Dry flat on a piece of dry newspaper then carefully peel off the top net. When dry, remove the bottom net. Press over a cloth with the iron set to 'silk'.

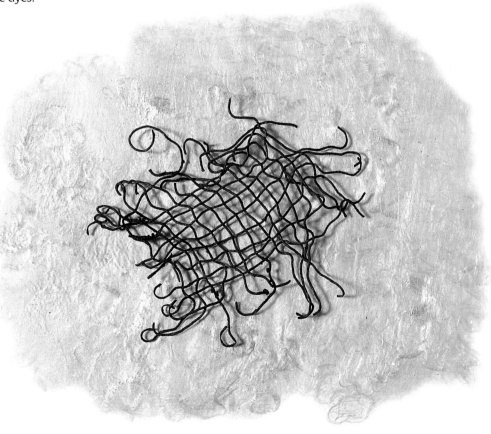

emboss
& water

Embossing is one of the simplest and most effective ways of creating an impression.
It is, in itself, the art of 'impressing' your paper with a design but it also produces smart and sophisticated results that will certainly impress your friends.

Provided your fresh paper is of a reasonable weight, it will happily accept any raised object or pattern you place beneath it. Leave it to dry and you will have created a relief image on the surface of the paper that can be as intricate as lace or as bold as chicken wire.

Using string as a medium, you could create monograms or abstract images that will effortlessly rise to the surface of your paper. Lace, feathers, coins and all manner of textured surfaces can be arranged in formal patterns or used as a single motif on the corner of a sheet of notepaper. If you are handy with a craft knife, you could make your own lino- or woodcuts with which to emboss your paper.

You could also create interesting seals with an oven-bake clay or go for an all-over effect by couching your paper on to a textured fabric such as basket weave or wire mesh. To prevent sticking, it is a good idea to coat any hard object with either a non-stick cooking spray or talcum powder before use. These will act as release agents and enable you to lift your paper cleanly off the object in question.

Another sophisticated method of personalizing your paper is with a watermark. This is a transparent image that shows through your paper when it is held up to the light.
A watermark is created by 'drawing' your design with wire or thread directly on to the surface of the screen of your mould. The design is then stitched in place so that it remains secure. Watermarks can be very intricate and pictorial or as simple as a fine border that could serve as a hallmark on all your paper compositions.

ing
marks

impressario

These papers show how even the finest lace can create an embossed surface on your paper. The indentation formed on the reverse side is equally attractive so you choose which is to be the 'right' side of the paper. Here, I have used the corner of a lace handkerchief and some sprigs of conifer, all impressed into pale, pastel-coloured pulps. Keep your eyes open for any lace trimmings and use these to create pretty embossed motifs or borders.

❏ Makes four A5 or circular sheets of one colour paper

approximately 40 g (1½ oz) dry waste note paper
    in pastel colours
water
15 g (1 tbsp) grated soap dissolved in boiling water
15 g (1 tbsp) cold water starch dissolved in ½ cup cold water
lace trimmings or ferns

additional equipment
circular sewing frame covered with curtain netting (if circular
    paper is required)
2 pressing boards 5 cm (2 in) larger than paper
4 G-clamps or heavy weights
couching cloths
newspaper
palette knife

Pulp your paper in separate coloured batches as described in the basic instructions on page 16. Place the pulp into the vat and add enough water to create the consistency of thin porridge. You'll need approximately 3 litres (5¼ pints). Now add the diluted soap and starch and stir gently to avoid making air bubbles.

Holding the deckle and mould (or sewing frame) vertically with the mesh facing you, dip them in the back of the vat bringing them up into a horizontal position. Holding them level, carefully lift the sewing frame (or deckle and mould) out of the pulp. Shake gently to disperse the fibre evenly, then allow to drain for about 20 seconds. Tilt the mould slightly and drain for 10 seconds more. Couch the paper on to a couching mound (see full instructions on page 17).

EMBOSSING: While the paper is still wet, position the item to be embossed on to the surface. Cover with a second, damp couching cloth, taking care to smooth out any wrinkles.

PRESSING: Pressing each paper individually, place the paper and cloths on to a pressing board (see full instructions on page 18). Cover with a second pressing board and weight down with a heavy object or tighten screw clamps on your press. Leave the papers for ten minutes and then increase the pressure. This pressing process is used to not only extract the excess water but also to firmly emboss the paper. It should take approximately half an hour in total.

Remove the top pressing board and carefully lift off the paper and cloths with the lace or ferns still in place. Leave to air dry for approximately 24 hours. When the paper is completely dry, press the back (with cloths and lace still intact) with a cool iron. Remove the couching cloths and embossing items. To increase the embossed effect, press once more pushing the tip of the iron into the indentations.

Coloured papers in ice cream pastels are embossed with scraps of lace to create unusual circular notelets.

string quartet

This sophisticated paper quartet provides you with stationery for every occasion. It would also make the perfect gift set. The envelope is made from reinforced paper. Its shape was taken from a standard shop-bought envelope which I opened out and used as a template.

❑ Makes two A5 sheets of one colour paper plus two A4 sheets for the envelope

approximately 60 g (2¼ oz) dry waste notepaper
   in pastel colours
water
15 g (1 tbsp) grated soap dissolved in boiling water
15 g (1 tbsp) cold water starch dissolved in ½ cup cold water

additional equipment
2 pressing boards 5 cm (2 in) larger than paper
4 G-clamps or heavy weights
couching cloths
newspaper
palette knife
oddments of rug hooking or a large mesh canvas
builders' scrim
PVC adhesive
standard, shop-bought envelope

Pulp your paper as described in the basic instructions on page 16. Place the pulp into the vat and add enough water to create the consistency of porridge. You'll need approximately 2.25 litres (4½ pints). Now add the diluted soap and starch and stir gently to avoid making air bubbles.

the writing paper and cards

Holding the deckle and mould vertically with the mesh facing you, dip them in the back of the vat bringing them up into a horizontal position. Holding the deckle and mould level, lift out of the pulp. Shake to disperse the fibres and drain for 20 seconds. Tilt and drain for 10 seconds more.

EMBOSSING: Couch the paper on to a couching mound. Cut oblongs and triangles from the rug hooking canvas and, bearing in mind that your images will be reversed, arrange them on the surface of the wet paper to form borders, patterns or corner motifs. Lay a damp couching cloth on the top.

PRESSING: Pressing each paper individually, place the paper and cloths on to a pressing board 5 cm (2 in) larger than the finished size of the paper, (see full instructions on page 18). Cover with a second pressing board and weight down with a heavy object or tighten screw clamps on your press. Leave the papers for ten minutes and then increase the pressure. The pressing process is used to extract the excess water and define the designs. It should take approximately half an hour in total. Remove the top pressing board and carefully lift off the paper and cloths with the canvas still in place. Leave to air dry for approximately 24 hours. When the paper is completely dry, press the back (with cloths and canvas still intact) with an iron set at 'silk'. Remove couching cloths and canvas. Cut into cards or trim edges for notepaper.

the envelope

Make one sheet of A4 paper as described and couch it on to a couching mound. Cover the surface with builders' scrim and then couch another sheet of paper directly on top. Now arrange your rug canvas offcuts into position working out where they will appear on the finished envelope (use the opened shop bought envelope as a guide). Cover with a damp couching cloth then press and dry as for the paper. Using the shop bought envelope as a template, cut and fold the paper, glueing down the edges with a PVC adhesive. The addition of the builders' scrim will add extra strength to the finished envelope.

Rug canvas has been used to create this linear design.

signature tune

To create a watermark in your paper, the design must be applied directly to your screen. This can be embroidered with thread or created from fine wire and then stitched into place. Another simple alternative is to 'draw' the design on to the mesh screen of your mould with a water-resistant glue — which is the method I have chosen here. The glue is difficult to remove from the screen after use so it would be wise to make up simple screens with old net curtaining specifically for these projects.

❑ Makes four A5 sheets of one colour paper

approximately 40 g ($1\frac{1}{2}$ oz) waste notepaper
water
15 g (1 tbsp) grated soap dissolved in boiling water
15 g (1 tbsp) cold water starch dissolved in $\frac{1}{2}$ cup cold water

additional equipment
2 pressing boards 5 cm (2 in) larger than paper
4 G-clamps or heavy weights
couching cloths
newspaper
palette knife
fine-nozzled tube of clear, waterproof adhesive
felt-tipped pen
plain paper

With the paper and felt-tipped pen, draw/trace the design you want to appear as a watermark. Place the drawing under the screen of your mould and draw over it directly on to the screen using a tube of glue. Set aside until completely dry.

Pulp your paper as described in the basic instructions on page 16. Place the pulp into the vat and add enough water to create the consistency of thin porridge. You'll need approximately 3 litres ($5\frac{1}{4}$ pints). Now add the diluted soap and starch and stir gently to avoid making air bubbles.

Holding the deckle and mould vertically with the mesh facing you, dip them in the back of the vat bringing them up into a horizontal position. Holding them level, carefully lift the deckle and mould out of the pulp. Shake gently to disperse the fibres evenly, then allow to drain for about 20 seconds. Tilt the mould slightly and drain for 10 seconds more. Remove the deckle.

COUCHING: Couch the paper on to a couching mound (see full instructions on page 17). Cover with a cloth.

PRESSING: Place the paper and cloths on to a pressing board 5 cm (2 in) larger than the finished size of the paper. (see full instructions on page 18). Cover with a second pressing board and weight down with a heavy object or tighten G-clamps on your press. Leave the paper in the press for ten minutes only. Remove the top pressing board and carefully lift off the paper and cloths. Leave to air dry for approximately 24 hours. When the paper is completely dry, press the back (with cloths still intact) with an iron set at 'silk'. Remove couching cloths.

improvisation

This is my jamming section. Here, you will find ideas that, for one reason or another, would not fit into my carefully composed chapters. As you will see from the photographs, I had a wild and wonderful time playing with fire, photocopies and funny teas that will turn your paper pretty colours and (to a minor degree) scent it at the same time. In addition, there are some inspirational ideas. I don't have room for full instructions for all the papers but there is nothing here that you cannot make from the general instructions in this book.

musical notes

If you are a person with musical aspirations you may well wish to include some notes with your notes. In a moment of impulse, I used an actual piece of sheet music for this paper. You could act more responsibly and use a photocopy for the same result.

❑ Makes one A4 sheet of paper

approximately 20 g ($\frac{3}{4}$ oz) dry paper (I used computer paper)
water
15 g (1 tbsp) grated soap dissolved in boiling water
15 g (1 tbsp) cold water starch dissolved in $\frac{1}{2}$ cup
   of cold water
sheet music or photocopy

additional equipment
2 pressing boards 5 cm (2 in) larger than paper
4 G-clamps or heavy weights
newspaper
palette knife

Pulp your plain paper as described in the basic instructions on page 16. Make a separate coarse pulp of the sheet music. Place the plain pulp into the vat and add enough water to create the consistency of thin porridge. You'll need approximately 3 litres (5$\frac{1}{4}$ pints). Now add the diluted soap and starch and stir gently. Add the sheet music pulp and stir once more.

Holding the deckle and mould vertically with the mesh facing you, dip them in the back of the vat bringing them up into a horizontal position. Holding them level, carefully lift the deckle and mould out of the pulp. Shake gently to disperse the fibres evenly, then allow to drain for about 20 seconds. Tilt the mould slightly and drain for 10 seconds more. Remove the deckle.

COUCHING: Couch the paper on to the prepared mound (see full instructions on page 17). Cover with a couching cloth.

PRESSING: Put a pressing board on top and weight down with a heavy object or place in press and tighten G-clamps. Leave the papers for ten minutes and then increase the pressure. The pressing process is used to extract only the excess water. It should take approximately half an hour in total.

Lift off the top pressing board and remove the paper with top and bottom cloths still attached. Peg up to air dry. When the paper is completely dry, press the back with an iron set at 'silk' to produce a smooth surface. Place under a pile of books for a minimum of 24 hours.

variation

Create a paper 'fragmented' with an old-fashioned musical score, Photocopy a whole sheet of music. Make up paper pulp as above and create a sheet of plain paper. Couch the paper on to the prepared mound (see full instructions on page 17). Place the photocopy face up on the newly made piece of paper. Cut strips of masking tape and lay these diagonally on the mould to cover the areas where you wish the photocopy to appear. Dip the mould back into the pulp to make a second piece of paper and couch this on top of the photocopy. Cover with a couching cloth. Press and air-dry as usual.

tea for two
(or three or four)

Tea bags are a very useful commodity as the leaves can be used to add texture and colour to your handmade paper. In addition, you can choose exotic flavours coupled with appropriate essential oils to complete the ultimate 'tea paper experience'. China tea, in particular, produces a heavily textured paper. Just for good measure I have thrown in some lemon zest paper and some mint paper – no tea involved, but lemon tea and mint tea are such delightful drinks I couldn't ignore them.

❏ Makes four A5 sheets of paper

approximately 40 g (1½ oz) dry good quality white paper
water
15 g (1 tbsp) grated soap dissolved in ½ cup boiling water
15 g (1 tbsp) cold water starch dissolved in ½ cup cold water
3 tbsp China tea
3 rosehip tea bags
handful of fresh mint leaves
handful of fresh lemon zest

additional equipment
2 pressing boards 5 cm (2 in) larger than paper
4 G-clamps or heavy weights
newspaper
palette knife

Place the China tea and the tea bags in separate containers. Cover with boiling water and leave to soak for half an hour. Boil up half the mint leaves in water. Dry remaining mint and lemon zest in a microwave for 3–4 minutes. Pulp your paper as described in the basic instructions on page 16.

Divide the pulp into four vats and add enough water to the vats to create the consistency of thin porridge. You'll need approximately 3 litres (5¼ pints). Now add diluted soap and starch to each vat and stir gently to avoid making air bubbles. Add half the china tea leaves to one vat, half the rosehip tea leaves, all the boiled mint and the dried zest to the others. Leave to soak for two hours. Add the remaining tea leaves and the dried mint to the appropriate vats. Make each sheet of paper separately using the following method:

Holding the deckle and mould vertically with the mesh facing you, dip them in the back of the vat bringing them up into a horizontal position. Holding them level, carefully lift the deckle and mould out of the pulp. Shake gently to disperse the fibres evenly, then allow to drain for about 20 seconds. Tilt the mould slightly and drain for 10 seconds more. Remove the deckle.

Leave to air-dry on the mould for approximately 24 hours. When the paper is completely dry, ease it off the mould. Press the paper with an iron set at 'silk' to produce a smooth surface. Stack the papers and place under a pile of books for a minimum of 24 hours. To make this paper extra special spray each sheet with an appropriate essential oil.

swan lake

A delicate and sophisticated paper with feathers and silver threads all floated on a sumptuous tissue paper base. Recycled tissue paper tends to produce 'crisp' results. I have added some soap both to keep the pulp soft and the finished paper pliable. Soap also acts as a sizing agent.

❑ Makes four A4 sheets or two A3 sheets of paper

4 sheets black tissue paper
2 tbsp grated soap dissolved in boiling water
water
fine silver thread
feathers (I've used white turkey feathers)

additional equipment
fine paintbrush or feather
palette knife

Pulp your paper as described in the basic instructions on page 16. Place the pulp into the vat and add enough water to create the consistency of thin porridge. Now add the diluted soap and stir gently.

Holding the deckle and mould vertically with the mesh facing you, dip them into the back of the vat bringing them up into a horizontal position. Carefully lift the deckle and mould out of the pulp. Shake gently to disperse the fibres evenly and then allow to drain for about 20 seconds. Tilt the mould slightly and drain for 10 seconds more. Set down on a flat surface and carefully remove the deckle.

Lay the silver threads across the surface of the pulp. Gently brush over the surface of the threads with a small paintbrush or large feather to adhere the thread to the pulp. Now arrange the feathers and secure the bottom of each quill with a small blob of wet pulp. Leave on the screen to air dry.

REMOVING THE PAPER FROM THE SCREEN: Once the paper is dry, run your fingers around the edges of the paper on the underside of the frame easing them up gently. This should release at least one corner of paper from the screen. Now slide the palette knife under a free corner and ease the paper off the mesh.

Press paper lightly on the reverse side with the iron set at 'silk'.

variation

*m*ake liquidized pulp from one sheet of silver tissue paper and put 30 ml (2 tbsp) into a small yoghurt container. Lay cut silver threads across the surface of the pulp. Dribble the silver pulp over the threads, making your own design. Lay the feathers into the silver pulp, securing with a blob of pulp at the bottom of each quill. Air-dry and release paper as described above.

crescendo

Interesting effects can be achieved by burning sections of your paper. Burnt edges give the impression of old parchment which can be rolled to form a scroll. You could also burn a design into the paper but do be sure your burnt line doesn't join at any point or the centre piece will fall away.

The paper shown on the left was burnt using a joss-stick. Work on a firm surface covered with a cloth and have a second cloth close to hand. Holding your paper up, touch it with the lighted joss-stick and then stop the burn spreading by placing the paper down on the cloth and dabbing it with the second cloth.

ensemble

Once you have created a range of papers you could use them in a collage. When composing a collage it is useful to think around a theme. This might be inspired by nature, industry, seashore, forest or whatever else comes to mind. Once your theme is determined you will find it easier to choose appropriate colours and textures to reflect it.

To begin the process, tear or cut your selected papers into interesting shapes and play with different arrangements, laying them on top or beside each other until the colours and textures harmonize. Consider adding loose fibres, leaves, fabric, seashells or any findings that fascinate you. Glue your composition on to a suitable board or background paper with PVA glue or stitch the pieces together with embroidery threads.

woodwind

Experimenting with the texture of handmade paper is as interesting and rewarding as the more obvious variations of colour, additives and scent. I have covered the use of many ingredients that will create texture but I have not, as yet, sung the praises of sawdust. This is a useful medium to add to your pulp and also to incorporate in your collage. When considering wood, think also of the lovely swirly pieces that result from planing.

Basic sawdust can be bought from a petshop but by creating your own you can control the texture. You can also make use of the many colours and tones of wood dyes and stains that are on the market. Sawdust can be applied to a collage using wet pulp as an adhesive, alternatively it can be scattered on to wet PVA glue.

stockists

UNITED KINGDOM

Deckles and Molds
The Paper Shed
March House
Tollerton
York YO6 2EQ
Tel: 01347 838253

Fibre Crafts
Style Cottage
Lower Eashing, Godalming
Surrey GU7 2QD
Tel: 01421853

Homecrafts Direct
PO Box 38
Leicester
LE1 9BU
Tel: 0116 251 3139
Fax: 0116 251 5015
Mail order crafts supplies, including
paper making equipment

General Fibres:
Angela Ramsay
Fron Isaf
Llanglydwen
Hebron , Whitland
Carms SA34 OJX
Tel: 01994 419523

Sue Harris
The Mill
Tregoyd Mill
Three Cocks
Brecon, Powys LD3 0SW
Tel: 01497 847421

Silk Fibres:
H.T. Gaddum & Co. Ltd.
3, Jordongate
Macclesfield

Cheshire SK10 1EF
Tel: 01625 427666
Also supplies hand dyed threads,
beads, fabrics and handmade papers.
Courses by arrangement

Wingham Wool Work
70, Main St
Wentworth
Rotherham, S. Yorks S62 7BR
Tel: 01226 742926

SOUTH AFRICA

Le Papier du Port
39A Gardens Centre
Mill Street
Gardens
Cape Town 8001
Tel/Fax: (021) 462-4796

Chat Noir
106 Fordyce Road
Walmer
Port Elizabeth 6070
Tel/Fax: (041) 51-1940

The Craftsman
Shop 10
Progress House
Bordeaux Drive
Randburg
Johannesburg 2194
Tel: (011) 886-0441
Fax: (011) 787-1846

Schweickerdt (Pty) Ltd
475 Fehrsen Street
Brooklyn
Pretoria 0181
Tel: (012) 46-5406
Fax: (012) 46-5471

L & P Stationery and Artists'
Requirements (3 branches)

Shop 10
College Square
Bloemfontein 9301
Tel: (051) 430-8608

AUSTRALIA

Paper Making Kits Australia
24 Connection Road
Pomona QLD
(07) 54852132

Pulp & Paper Connections
1 Headsail Drive
Banksia Beach QLD 4507
(07) 3408 8228

NEW ZEALAND

BJ Ball Papers
395 Church Street
Penrose
Tel: (09) 579 0059

The Paper House
7 Carmont Place
Mt Wellington
Tel: (09) 27 2683

further reading

Making Your Own Paper –
Marianne Saddington (New Holland)

The Art and Craft of Papermaking –
Sophie Dawson (Aurum Press)

Plant Papers – Maureen Richardson
(self published)

Creative Handmade Paper –
David Watson (Search Press)

index